by

Carla DuPont, Cameron Alexa, & Chase Huger

OTHER CHILDREN'S BOOKS BY CAMERON ALEXA

www.yayagirlz.com

About Black Culture Letter Tracing Alphabet Workbook

Published by About Black Culture, LLC

ISBN: 979-8-9860080-2-8

For bulk or school orders, email: orders@yayagirlz.com

Illustrations: Garrett Myers

This book belongs to:

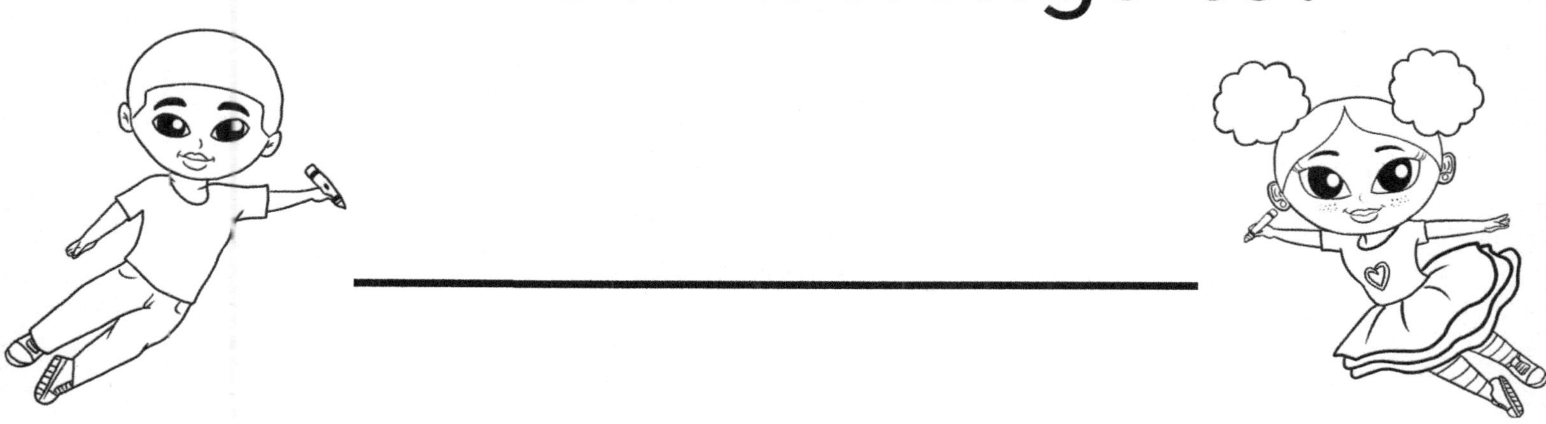

We want to give a shout out to these dope souls who've helped us bring this book to life!

Andrea Cobb-McMullen
Carl F. DuPont, Sr.
Christopher Pennix
Constance Poitier
Dr. Carl F. DuPont, Jr.
Elektra Thompson
James Poitier
Ja'Qonna Mathis
John McGhee, II
Kaliyah Hudson
Katrina Alexander
Michael Bonner
Monica DuPont
Natalie Jeanty
Pierre Alex Jeanty
Richard Sparks
Robert Thomas
Shermeka Raing

...And to our illustrator who painstakingly drew every illustration by hand...Garrett Myers, we love you!

Welcome to

About Black Culture Letter Tracing Alphabet Workbook!

We wanted to introduce kiddos to writing, but we wanted to do it in a dope way. What better than to teach Black culture at the same time! Instead of the usual apples and ants to illustrate the letter 'a', we have ankh, Africa, and Alvin Ailey. We blend hip-hop, fashion, pop-culture, inventors, and good ol' cultural favorites. This is an epic way to teach the alphabet.

Part 1...

Here, kids will learn how to write letters by tracing them. Then, they'll see cool, hand-drawn Black culture images that bring the alphabet to life. 'B is for...' you name it, we got it. They will see the alphabet in a way they've never seen it before. So will you!

Part 2...

Think Black history 365. That's where you're heading. Diving deeper than just pictures, you and your littles will do lit activities to build on the Black history they've just learned. Y'all can explore together.

Enjoy! And please leave us a review!

xo,
Carla, Chase, & Cameron

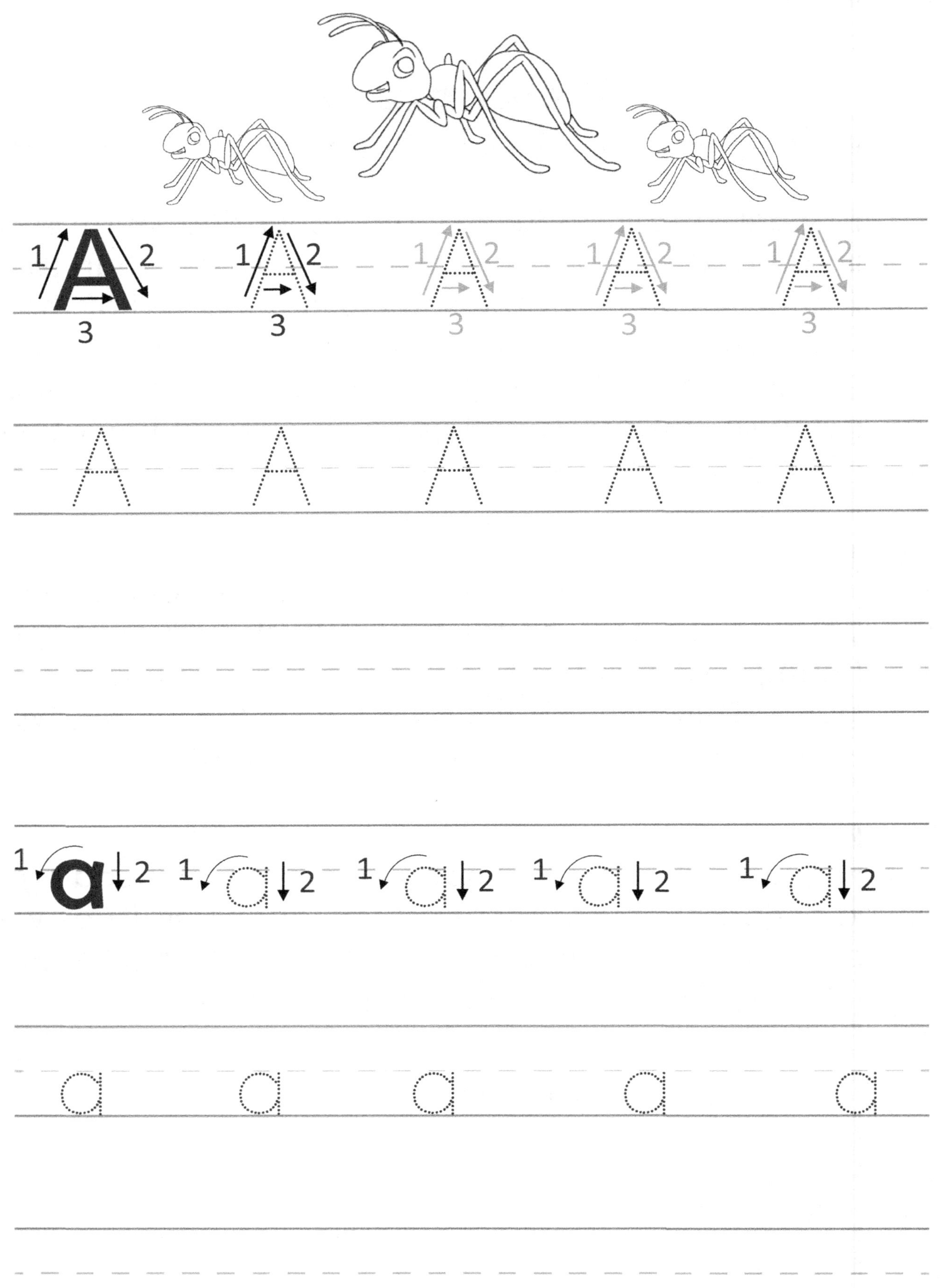
1
2
3
1
2
3
1
2
3
1
2
3
1
2
3
1
2
1
2
1
2
1
2
1
2

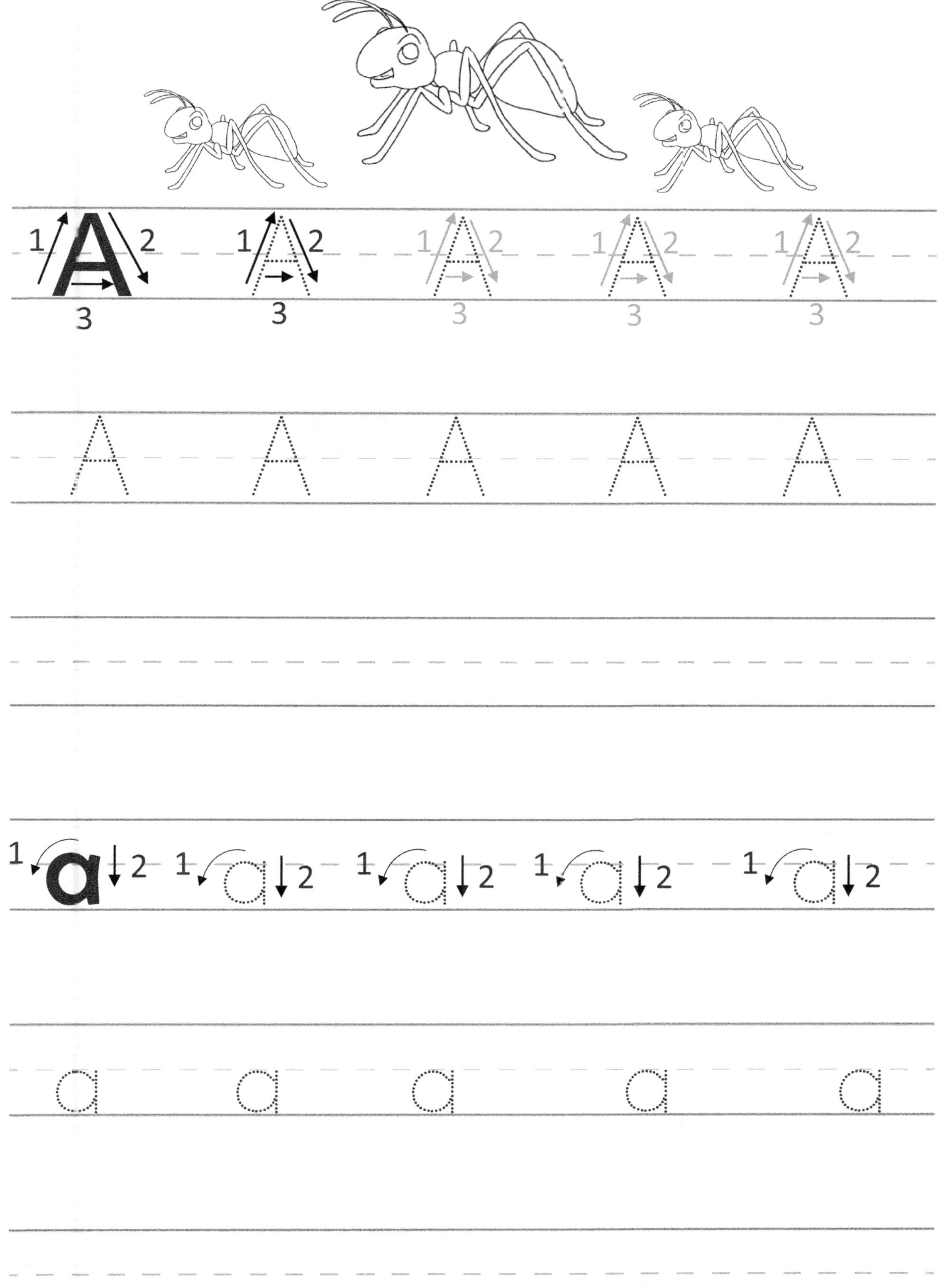
1 A 2
3
1 A 2
3
1 A 2
3
1 A 2
3
1 A 2
3
A A A A A
1 a 2
1 a 2
1 a 2
1 a 2
1 a 2
a a a a a

Ankh

Egyptian Symbol of Life

Ava Duvernay

Filmmker, TV Producer

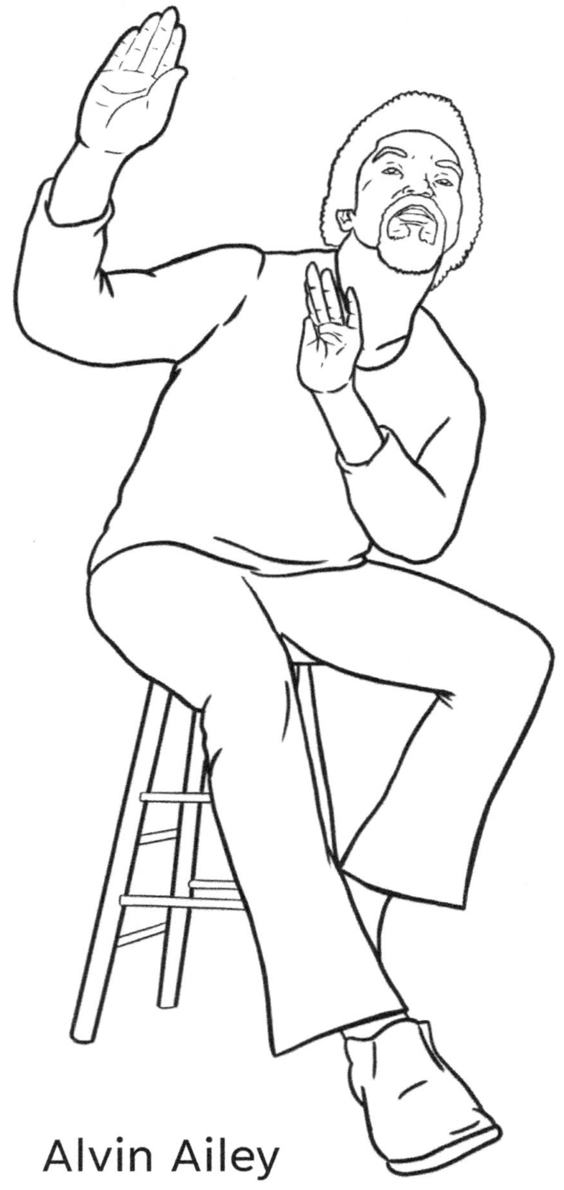

Alvin Ailey

Choreographer, Dancer, Director

Atlanta

U.S. City with 2nd Highest Black Population

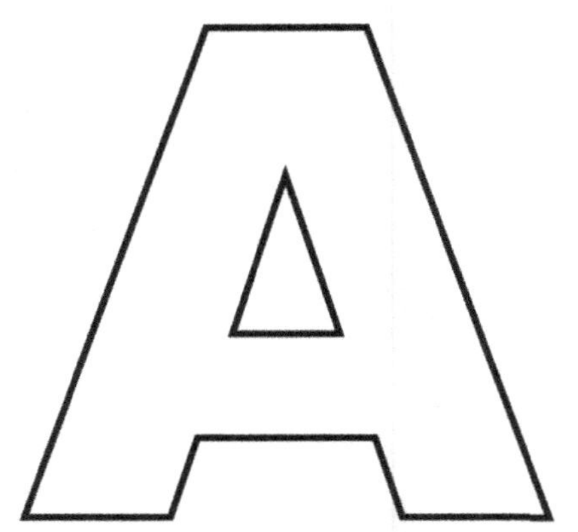

Althea Gibson
Pro Tennis & Golf Player
Afro
Africa
1 of 7 Continents
a
Arthur Ashe
Pro Tennis Player

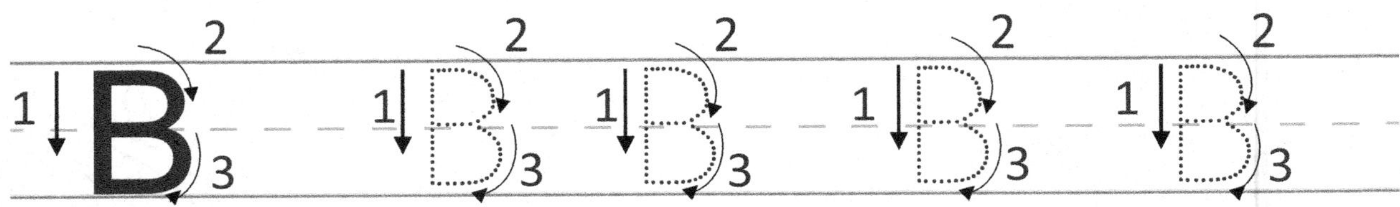

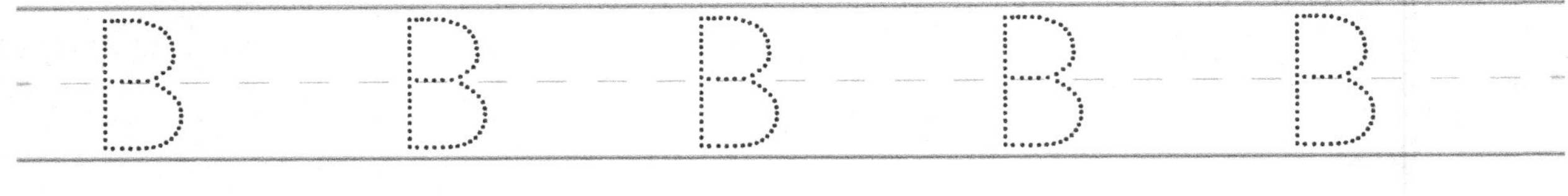

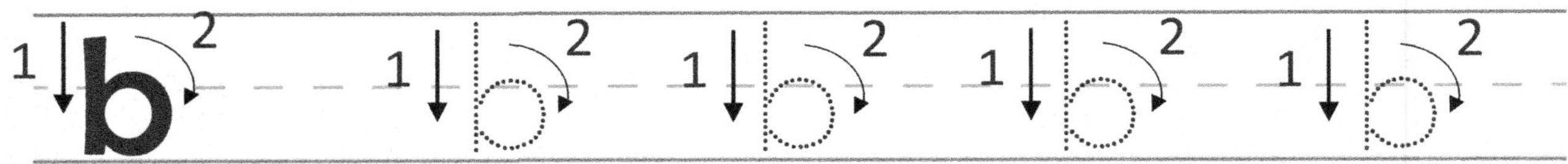

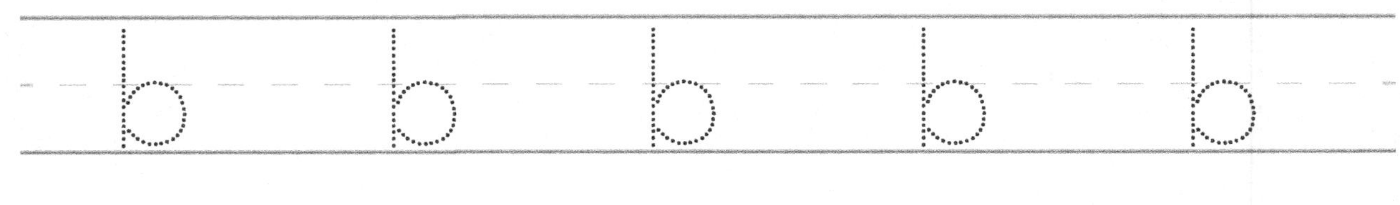

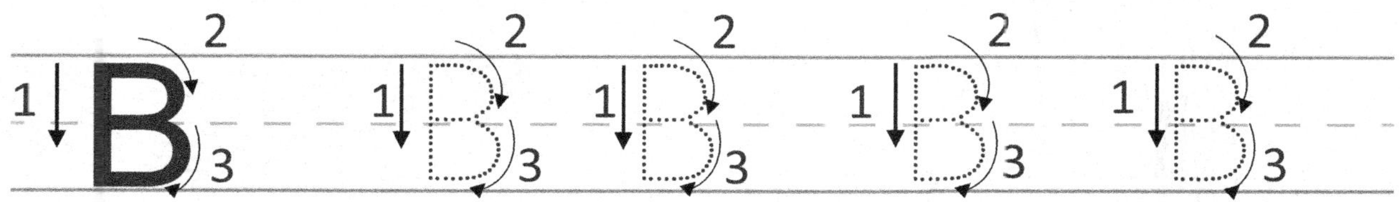

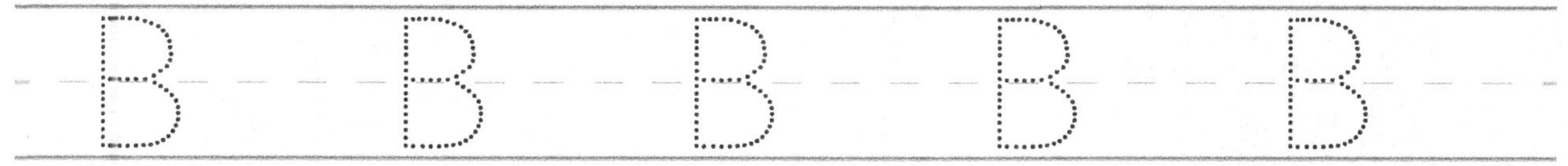

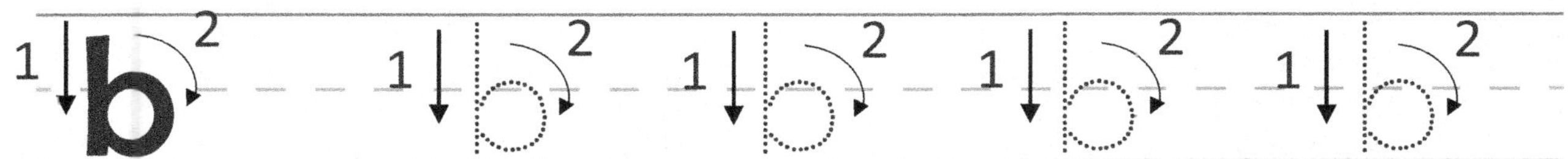

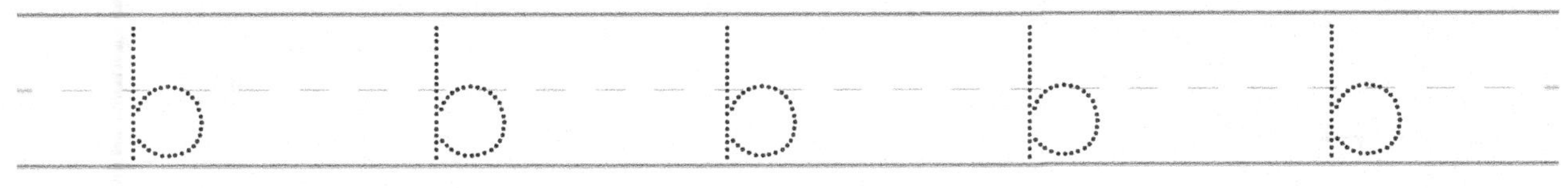

Beyonce

Singer, Songwriter, Actress

Black Panther Party

Bamboo Earrings

Banana Pudding

Black-eyed Peas

b

Bootsy Collins

Bass Guitarist, Singer

1 C C C C C

C C C C C

1 c 1 c 1 c 1 c 1 c

c c c c c

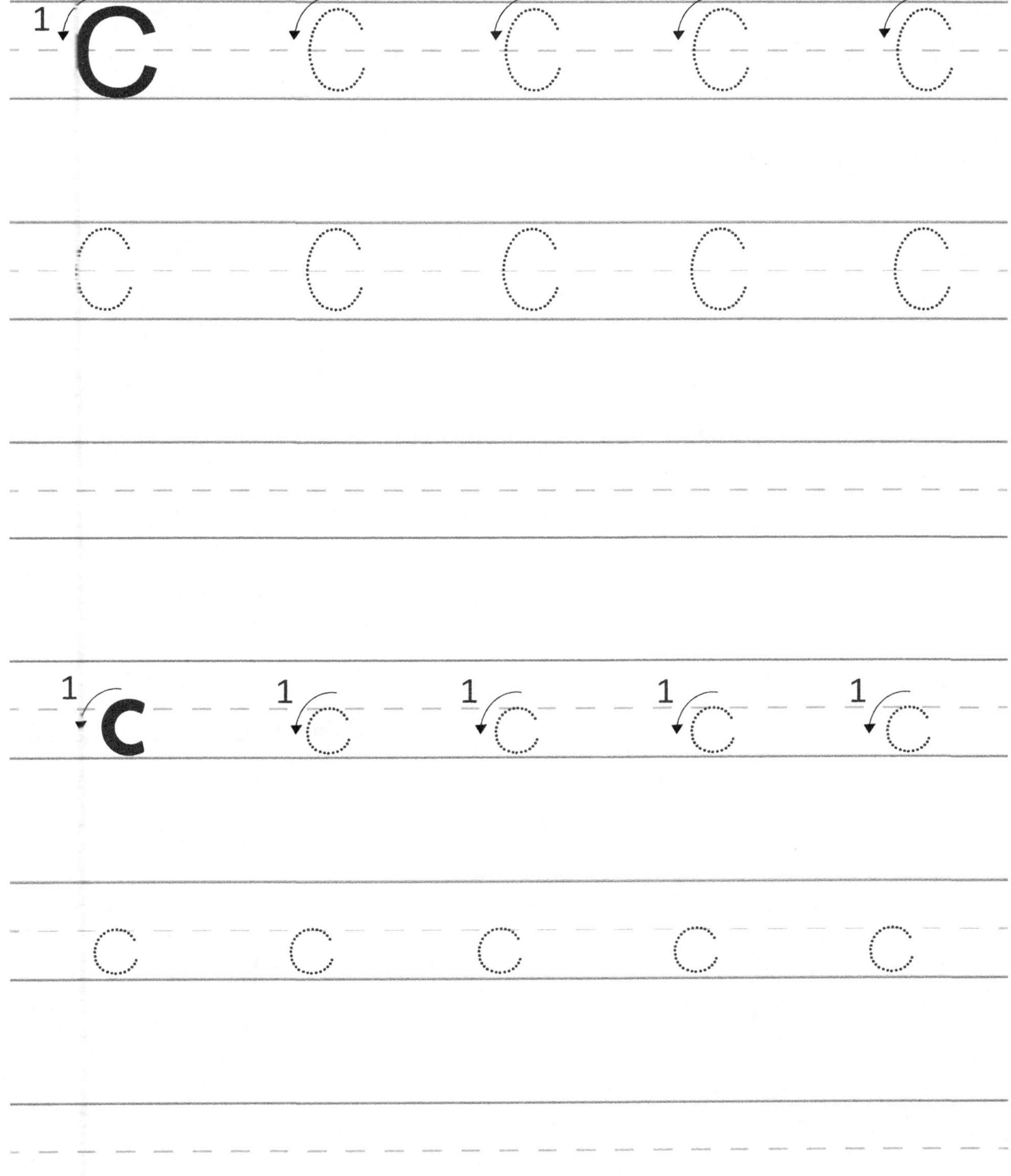

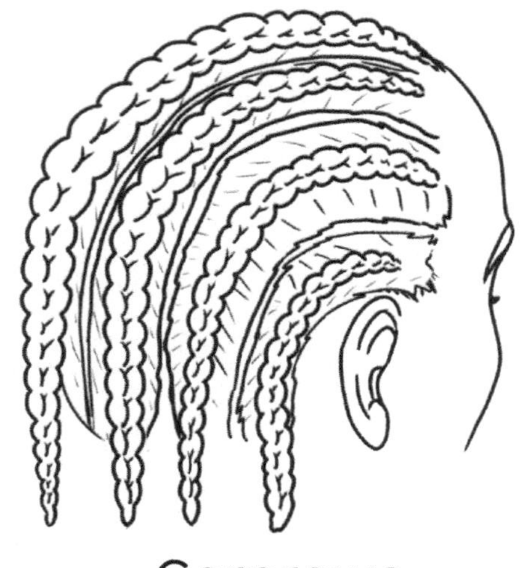

Cornrows

Chicken & Waffles

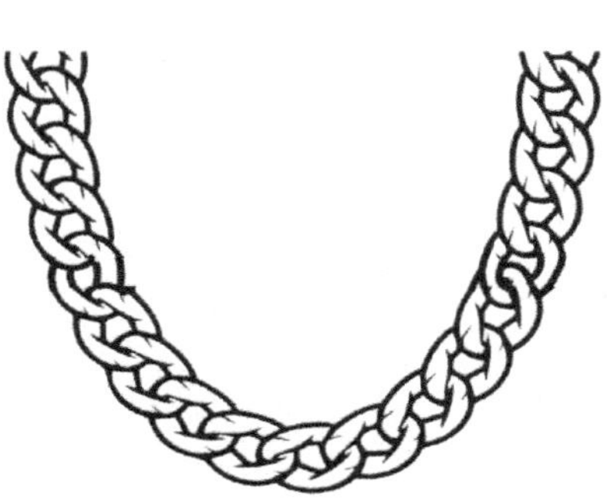

Chain

Chance The Rapper

Rapper, Singer-Songwriter

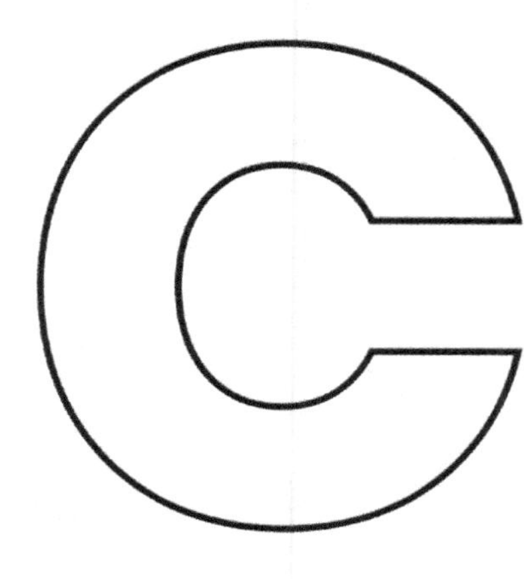

Cardi B

Rapper, Songwriter

Cornbread
Church
Chaka Khan
Singer, Songwriter
C
Coretta Scott King
Freedom Fighter, Opera Singer

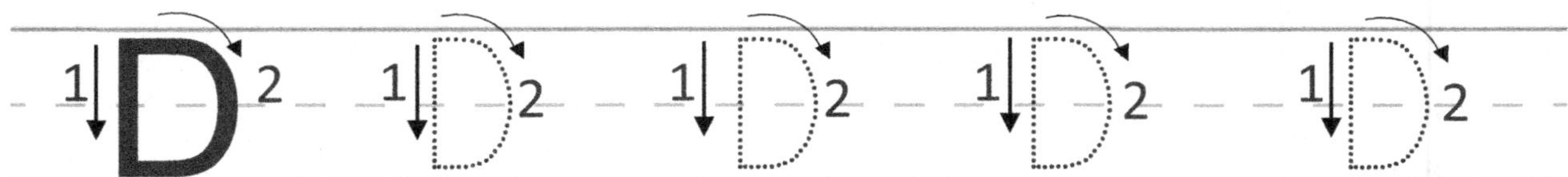

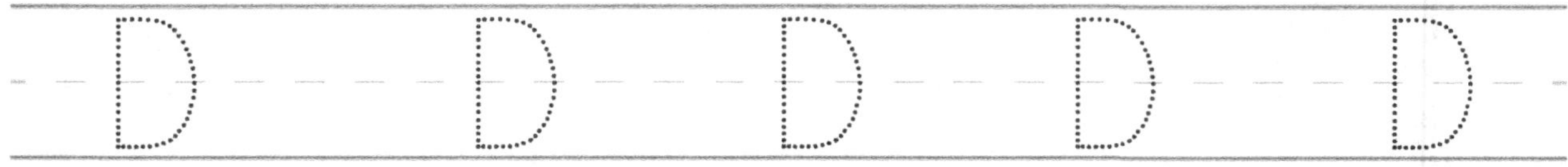

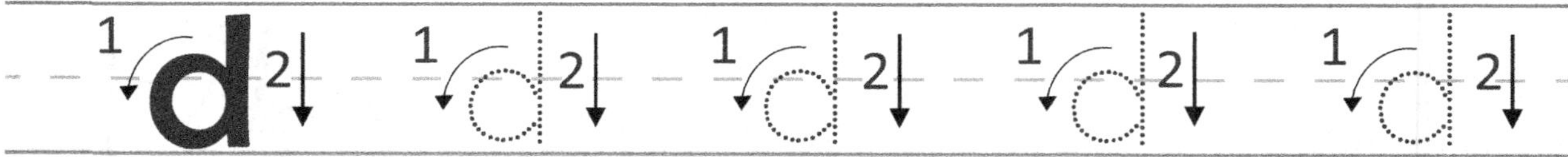

d d d d d

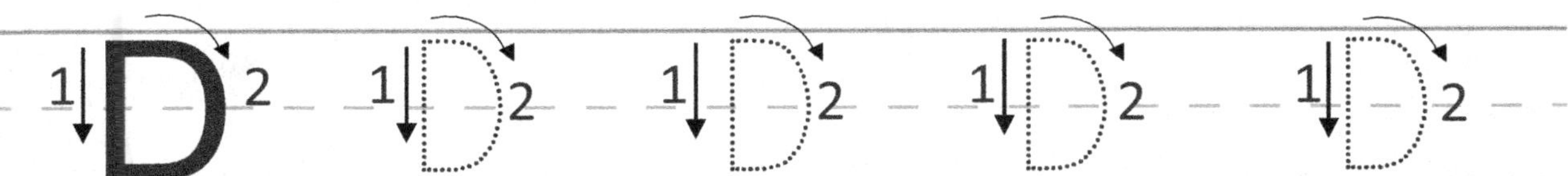

D D D D D

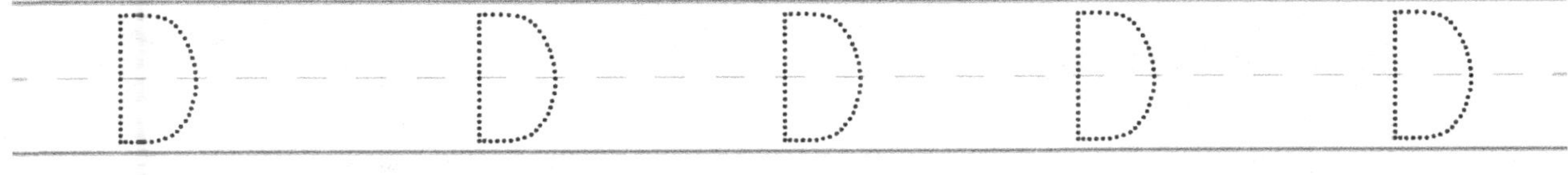

1 d 2
1 d 2
1 d 2
1 d 2
1 d 2

d d d d d

Double Dutch

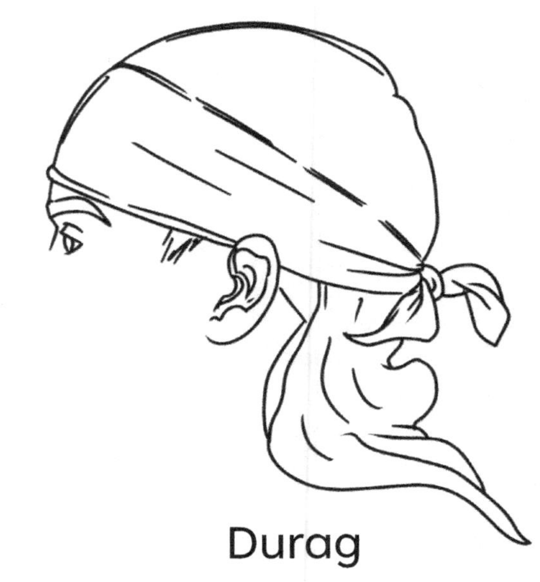

Durag

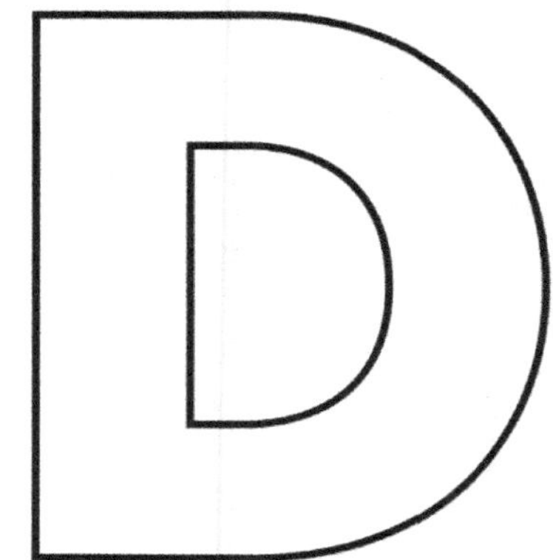

Djembe

(gem-bay)

Drum

D

Denzel Washington

Actor, Filmmaker

Dorothy Dandridge

Actress, Singer, Dancer

Dashiki

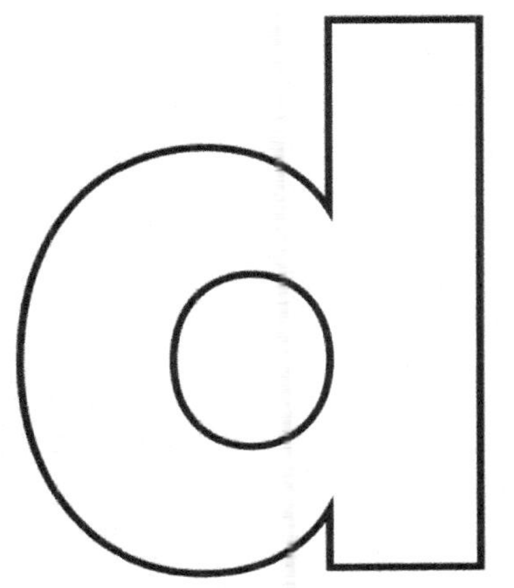

Dominoes

Game

Dap

Greeting

Drum Major

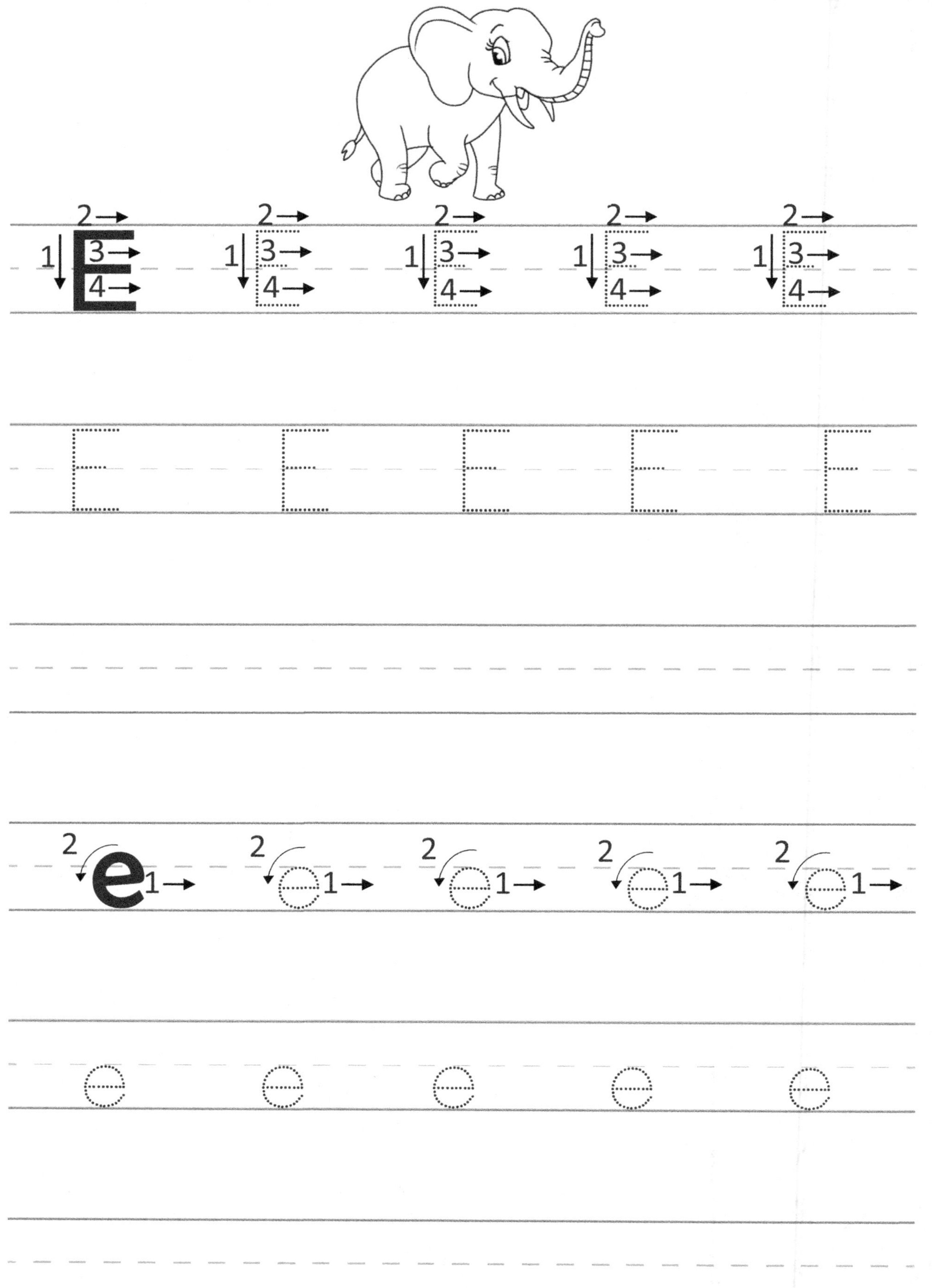

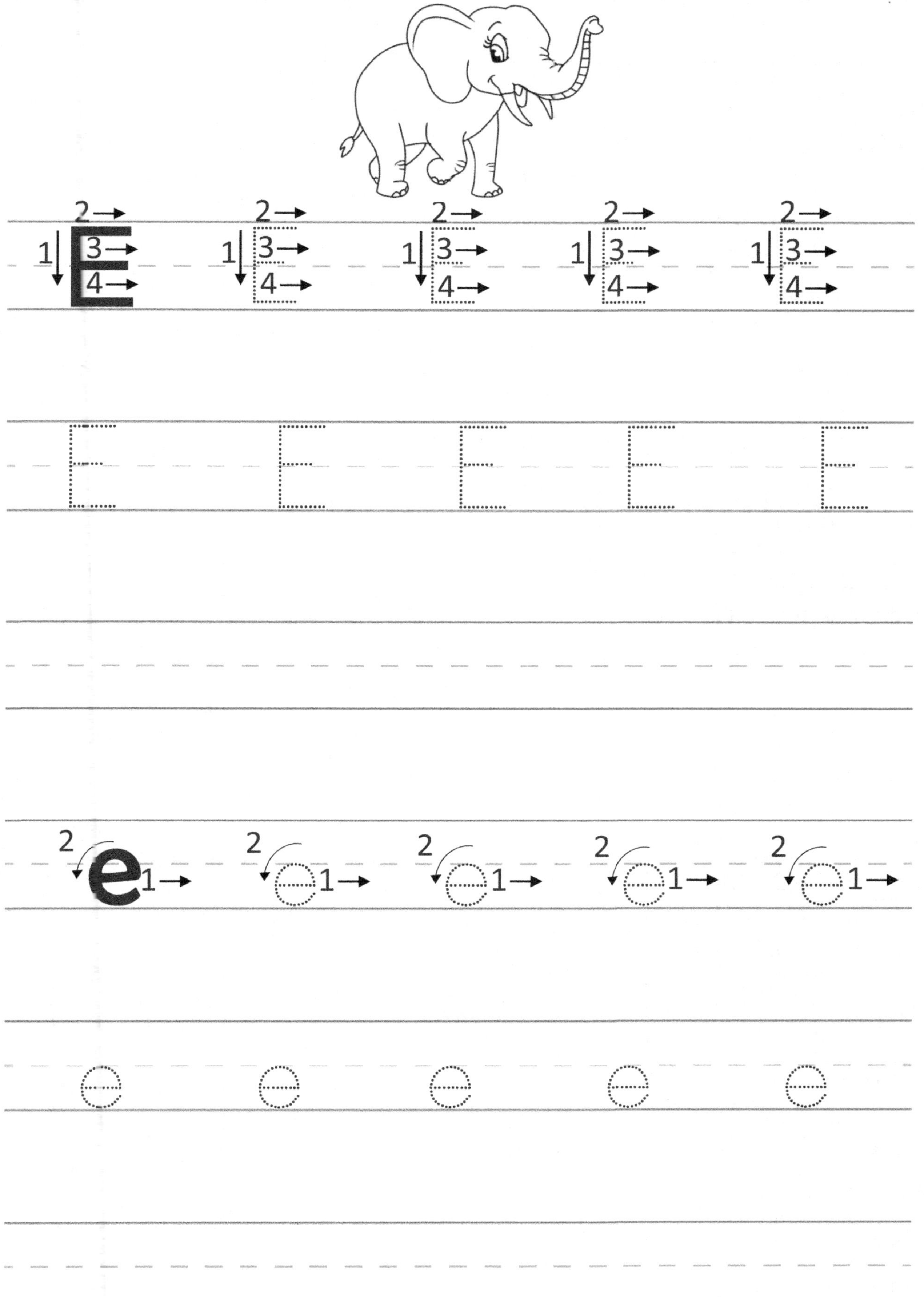
2→
1↓ E 3→
4→
e 1→
2

Ebony Magazine

Magazine Celebrating Black Culture

Eddie Robinson

Legendary Football Coach

Egypt

Country in Africa

Elijah McCoy

Engineer, Inventor

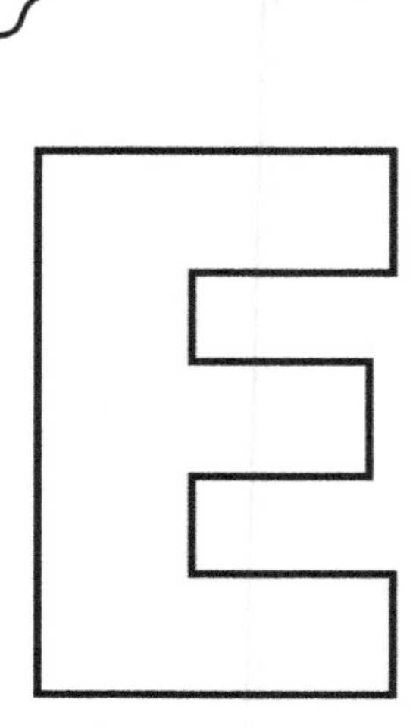

Erin Jackson

Speed Skater, Olympic Gold Medalist

Ella Baker

Freedom Fighter, Organizer

Eddie Murphy

Stand-up Comedian, Actor, Singer

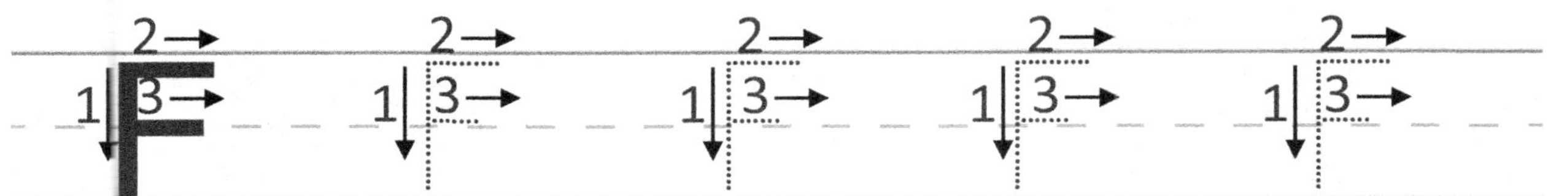

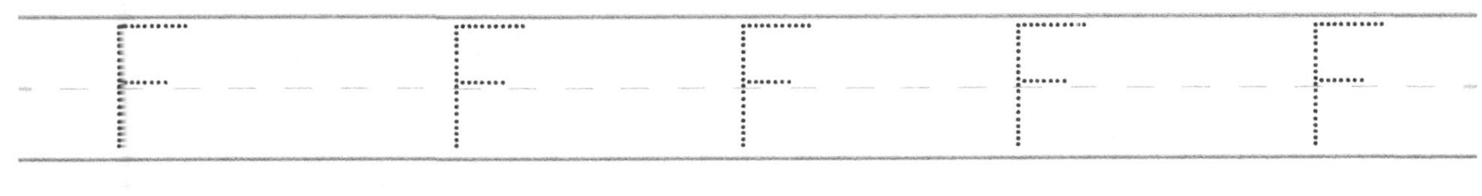

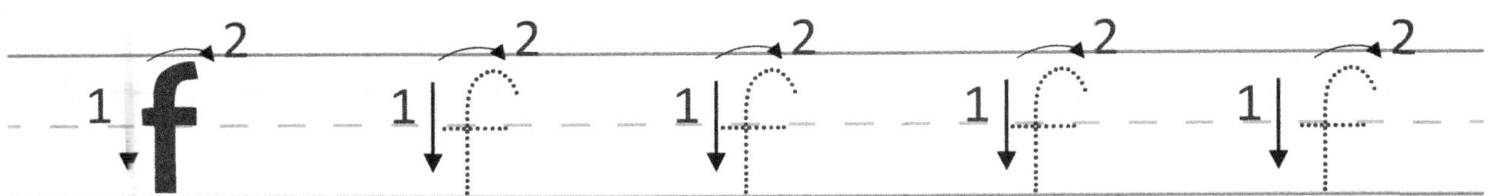

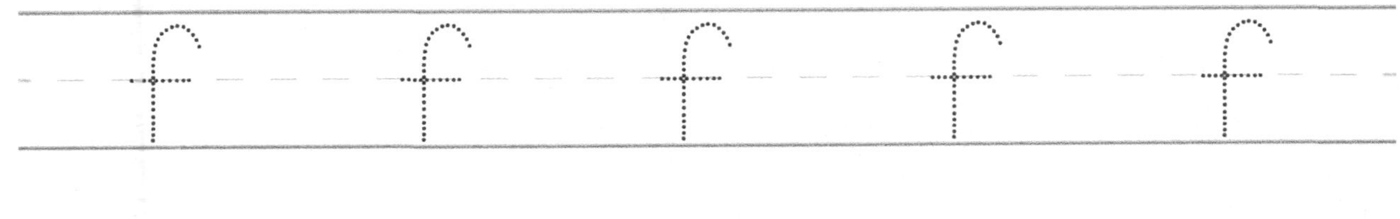

Fist Bump

Greeting

FUBU Clothing

For Us, By Us Clothing Brand

Flo-Jo

Track Star, Olympic Gold Medalist

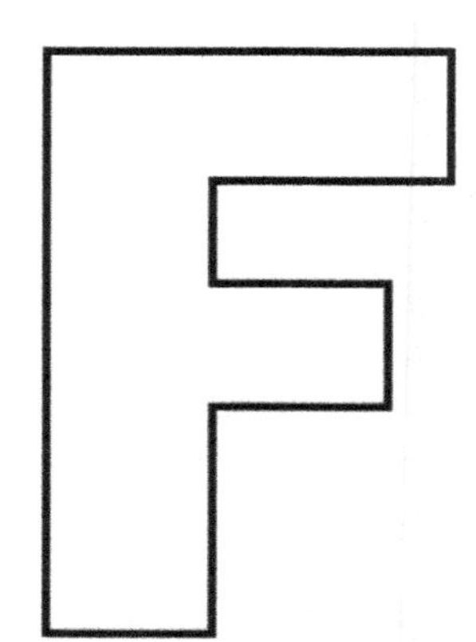

Freedom

February						
Sunday	Monday	Tuesday	Wednesday	Thursday	Friday	Saturday
1	2	3	4	5	6	7
8	9	10	11	12	13	14
15	16	17	18	19	20	21
22	23	24	25	26	27	28

February

Black History Month

Frederick Douglass

Freedom Fighter, Speaker

Fade

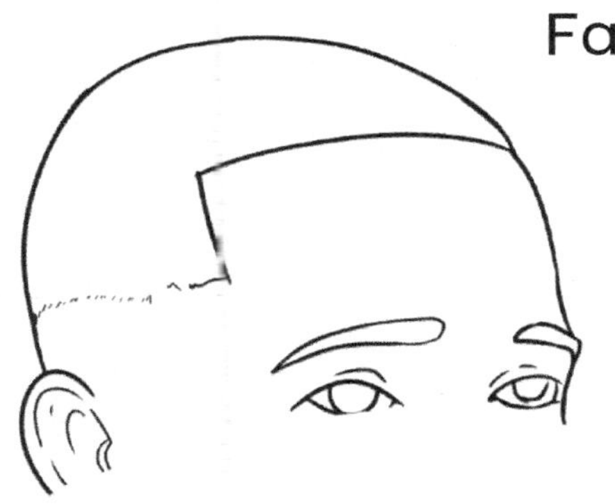

Fat Albert

1970's Cartoon Character

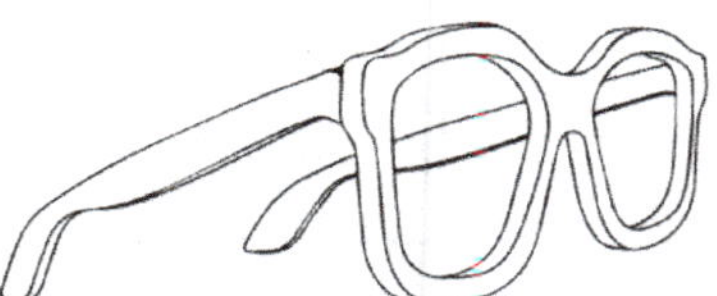

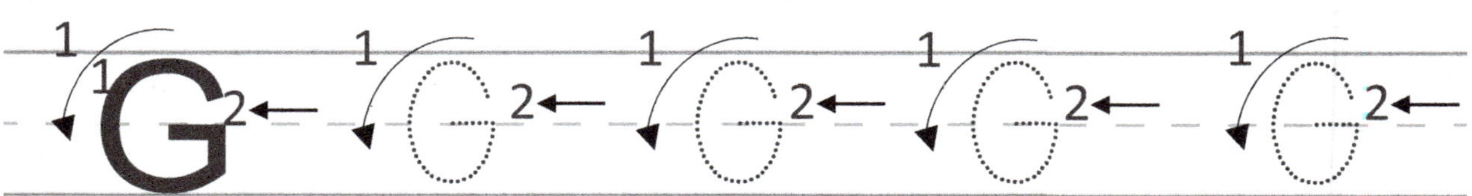

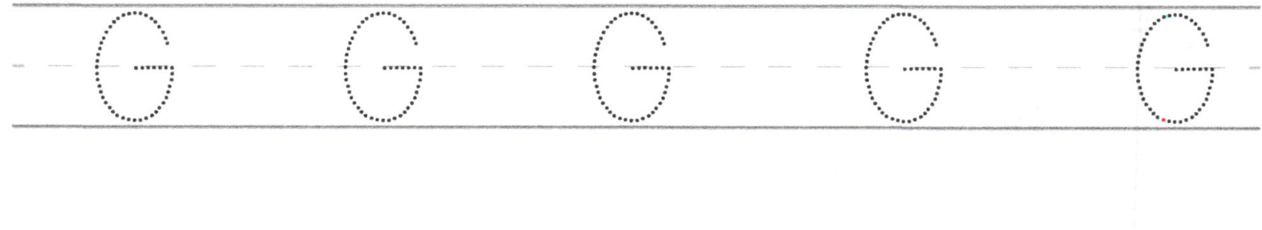

1 g 2

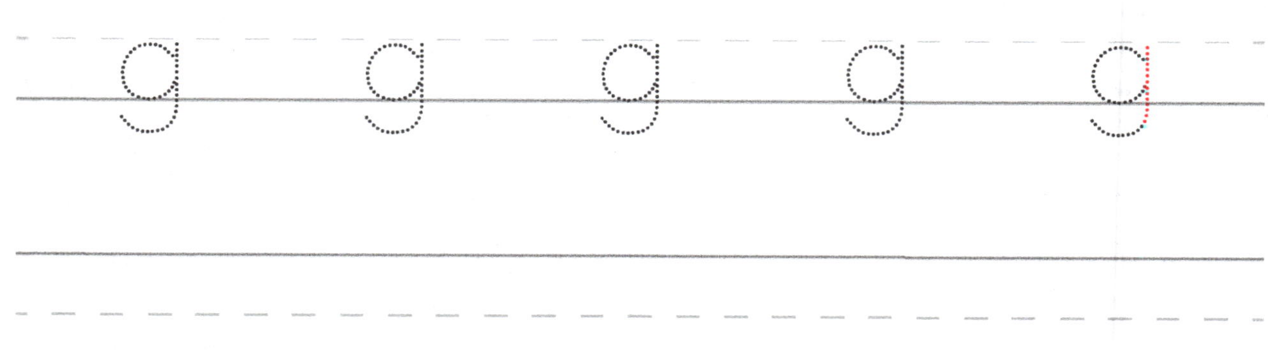

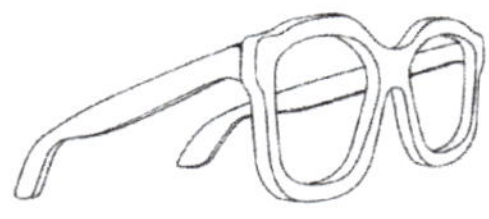

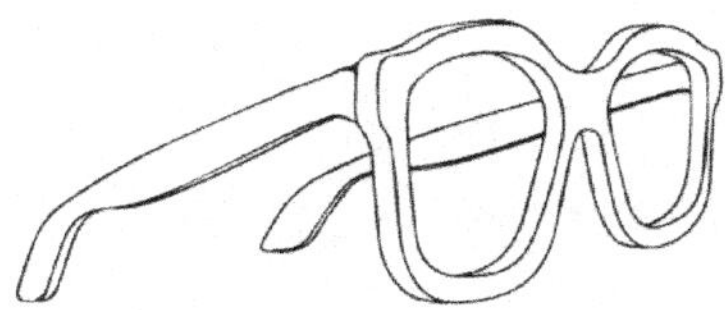

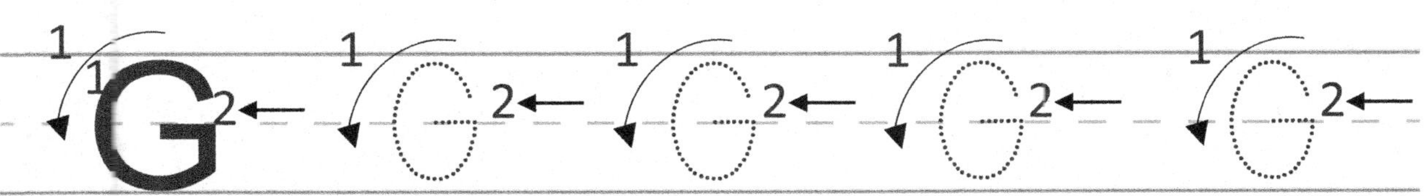

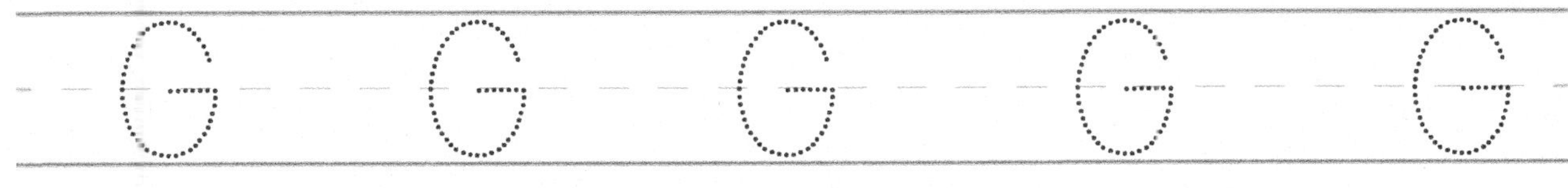

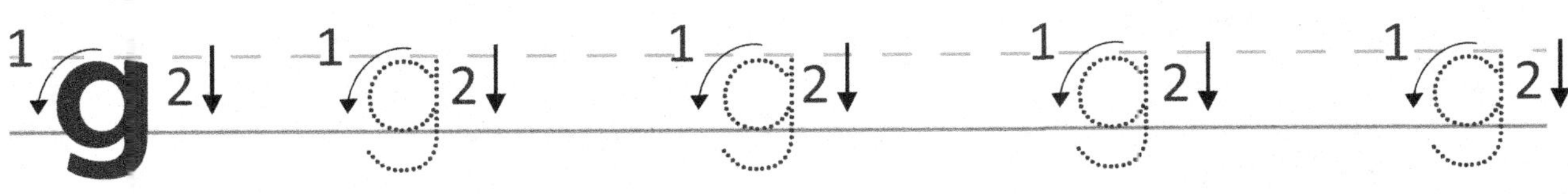

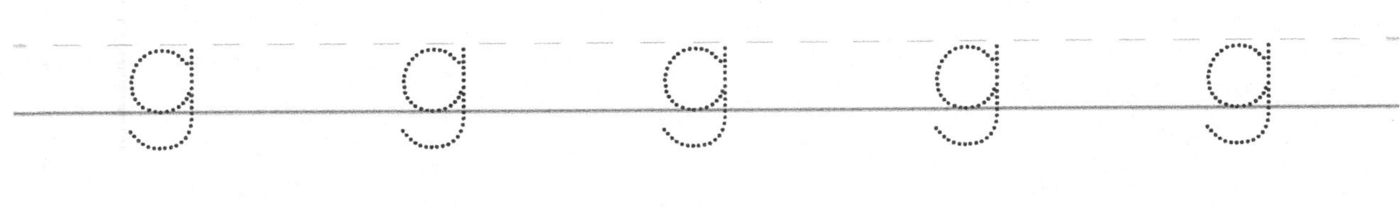

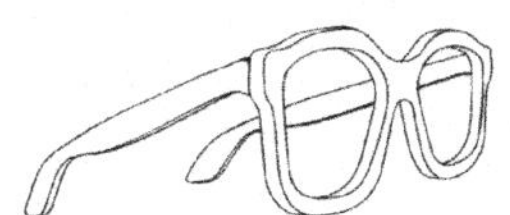

Gospel Choir

Gumbo

Gabby Douglas

Gwendolyn Brooks

Pulitzer Prize Poet, Author, Teacher

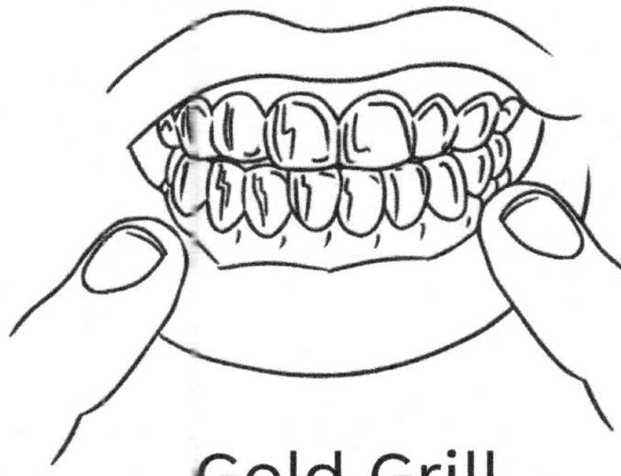

Gold Grill

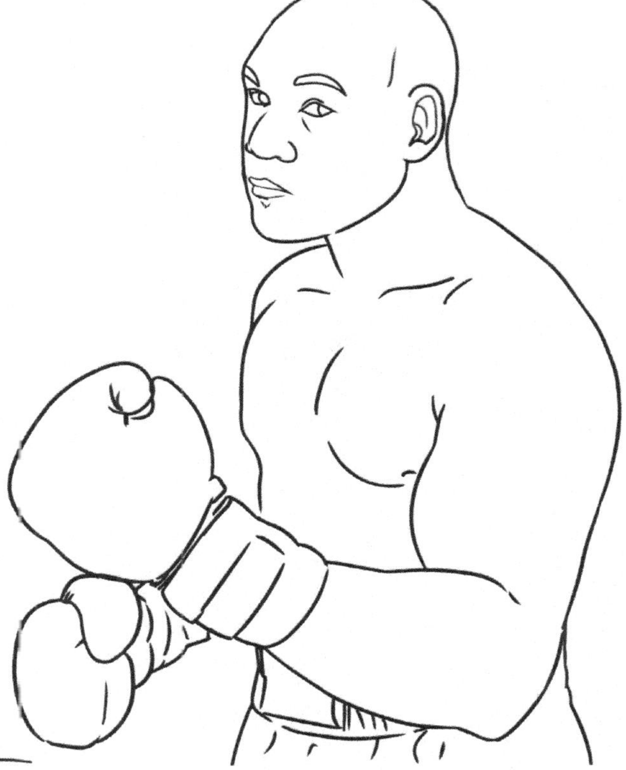

George Foreman

Professional Boxer, Business Owner

Grandmaster Flash

Trailblazing Hip-Hop DJ

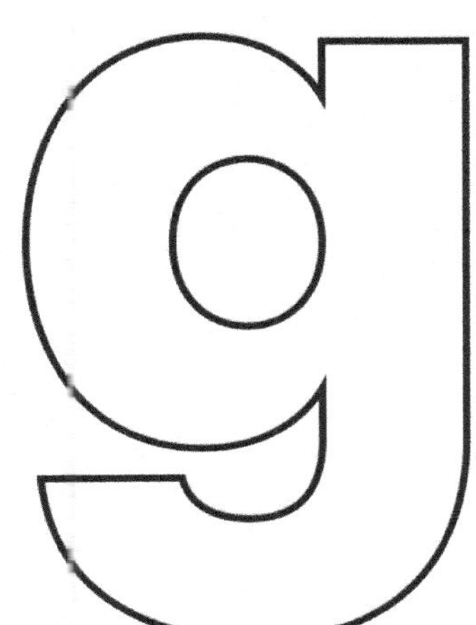

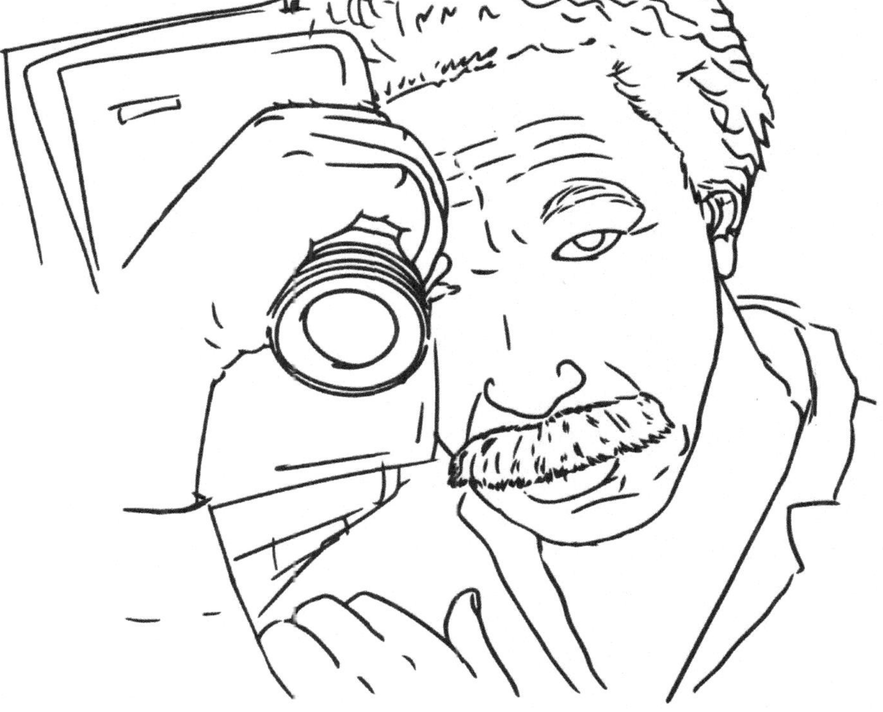

Gordon Parks

Photographer, Writer, Film Producer

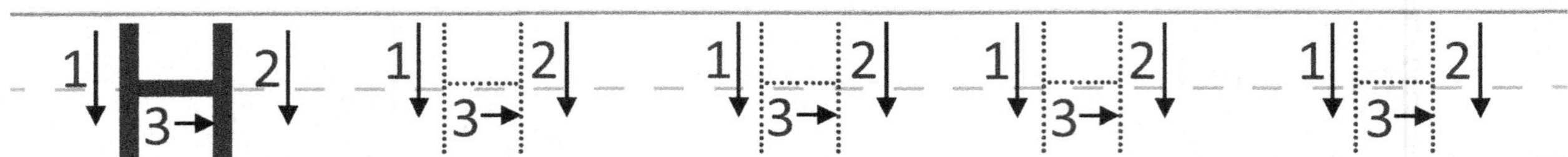

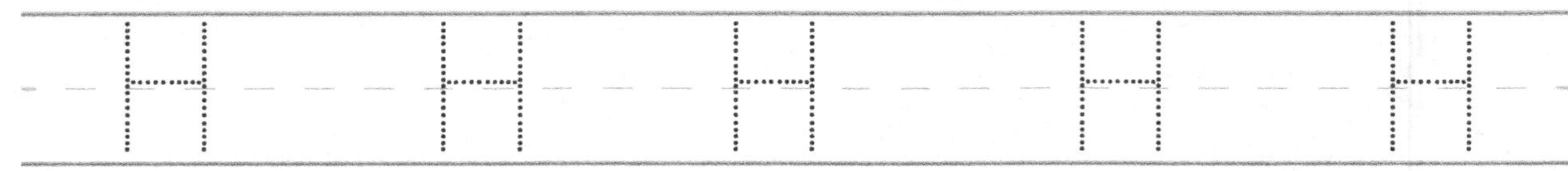

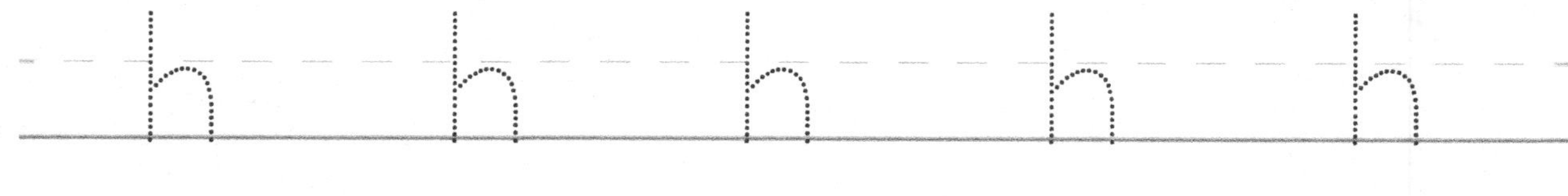

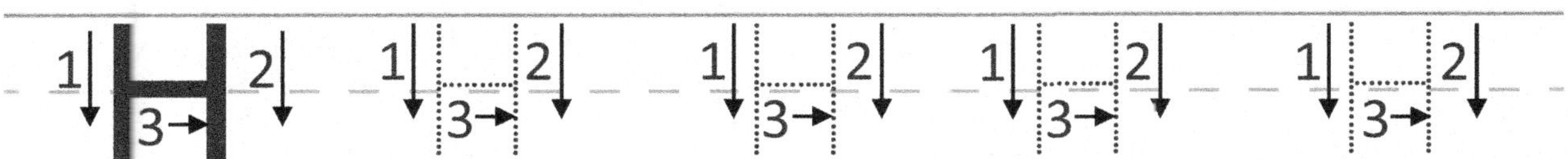

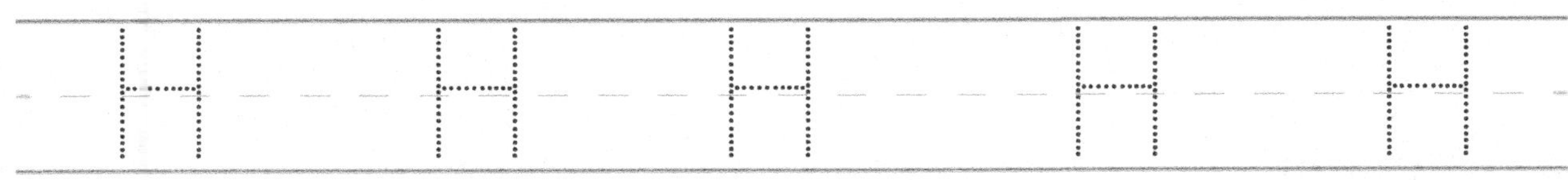

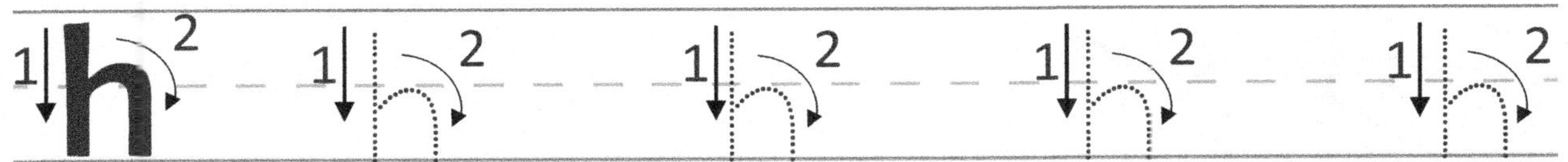

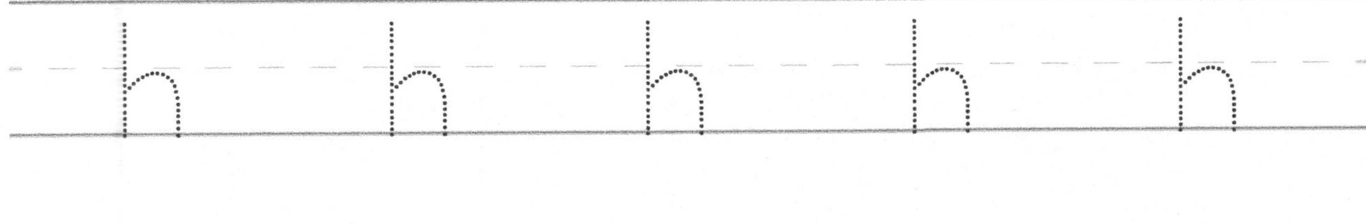

Harriet Tubman

Community Organizer, Women's Rights Activist

Hiram Revels

1st Black Man to Serve in Congress

Hair Grease

Hip Hop

Hair Bonnet

Hot Sauce

Flag of Haiti

1st Free Black Republic

Hot Comb

High-top fade

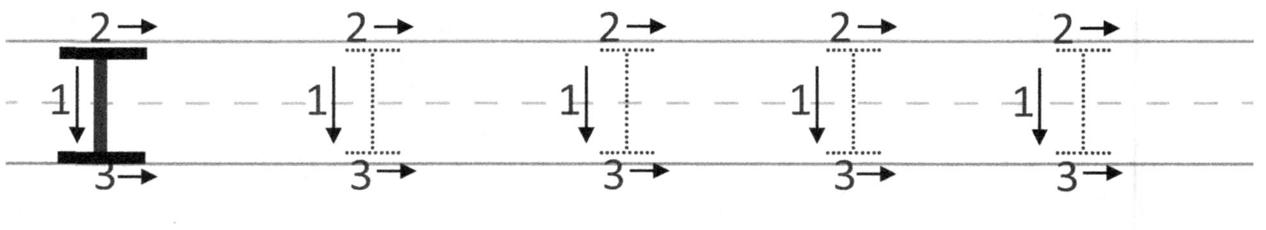

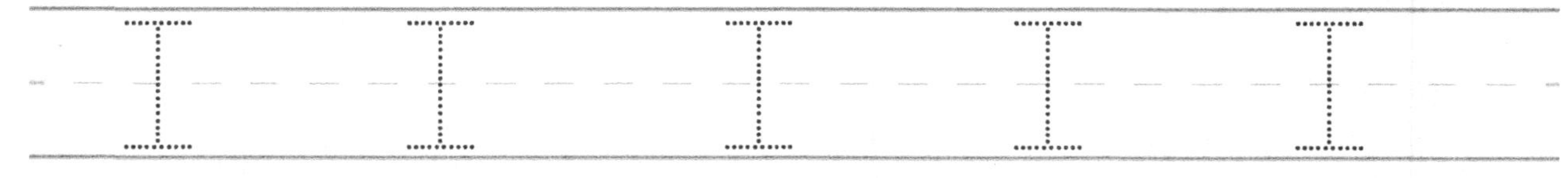

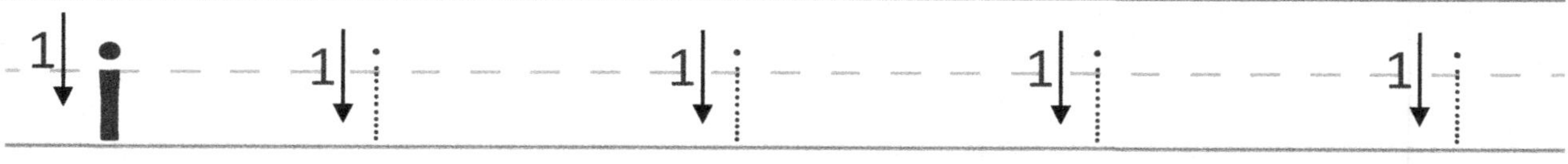

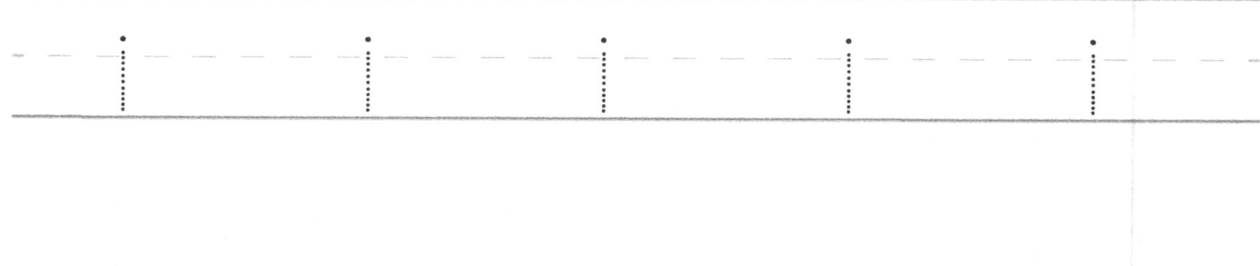

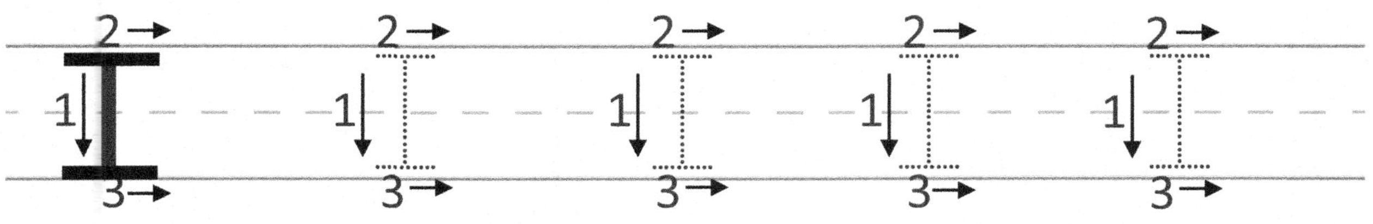

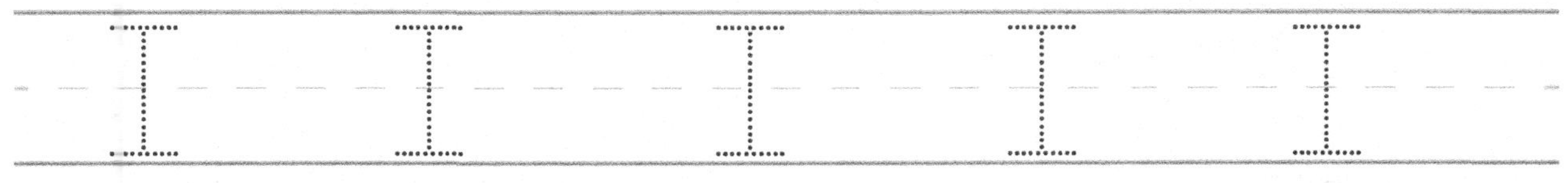

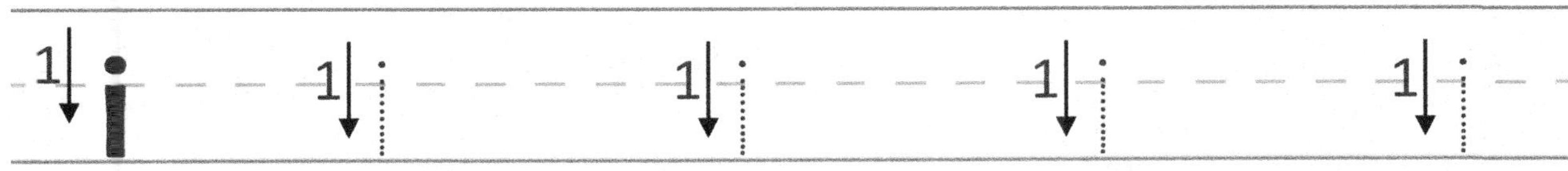

Issa Rae
Actress, Writer, Comedian
Ice Cube
Rapper, Actor, Filmmaker
Ida B. Wells
Freedom Fighter, Fact Finding Writer

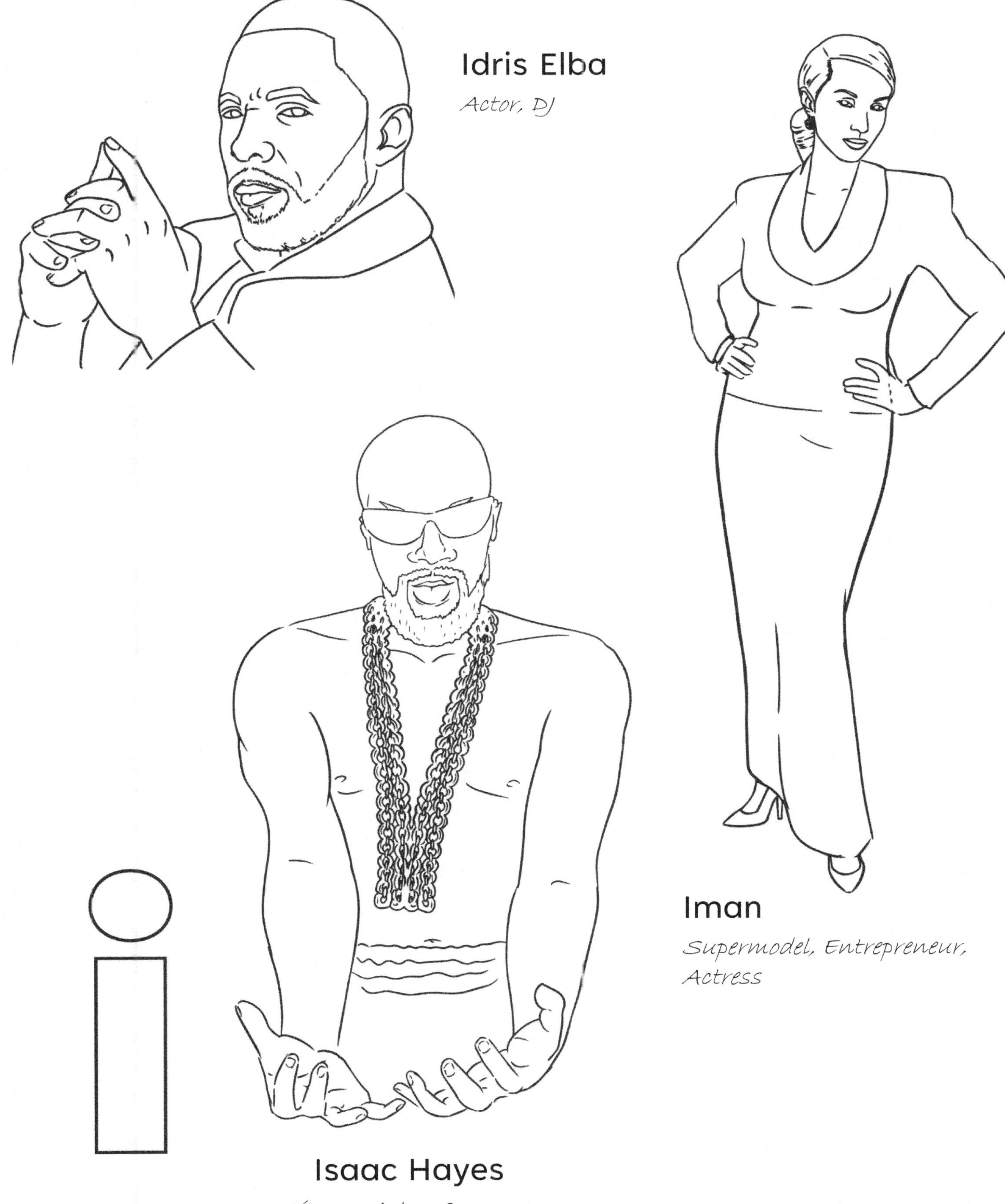

Idris Elba

Actor, DJ

Iman

Supermodel, Entrepreneur, Actress

Isaac Hayes

Singer, Actor, Composer

J 2→ 1↓ J 2→ 1↓ J 2→ 1↓ J 2→ 1↓ J 2→ 1↓

J J J J J

j 1↓ j 1↓ j 1↓ j 1↓ j 1↓

j j j j j

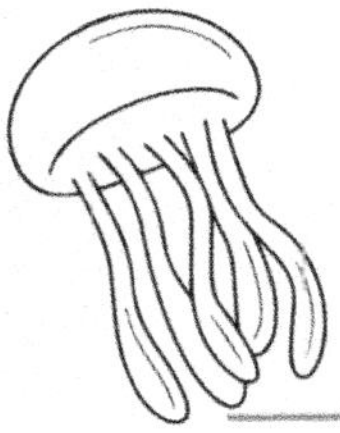

2→ J 1↓ 2→ J 1↓ 2→ J 1↓ 2→ J 1↓ 2→ J 1↓

J J J J J

j 1↓ j 1↓ j 1↓ j 1↓ j 1↓

j j j j j

Jumping The Broom

Wedding Ceremony

John Henry

American Legend

Jazz

J

James Brown

Singer, Dancer, Band Leader

JUNETEENTH

National Holiday

JET Magazine

Magazine Celebrating Black Culture

Josephine Baker

Dancer, Singer, Actress

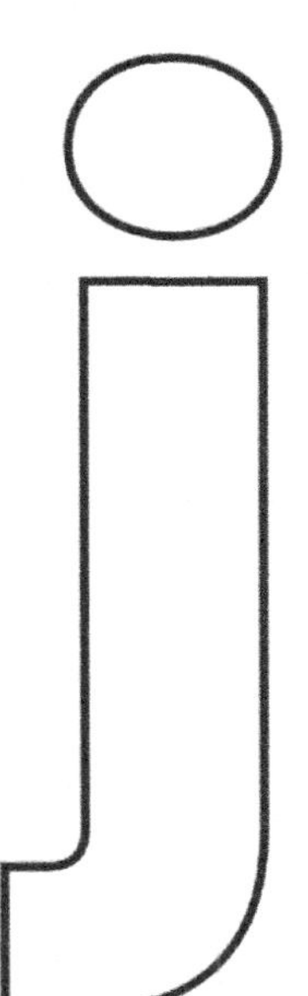

Jean-Michel Basquiat

Artist

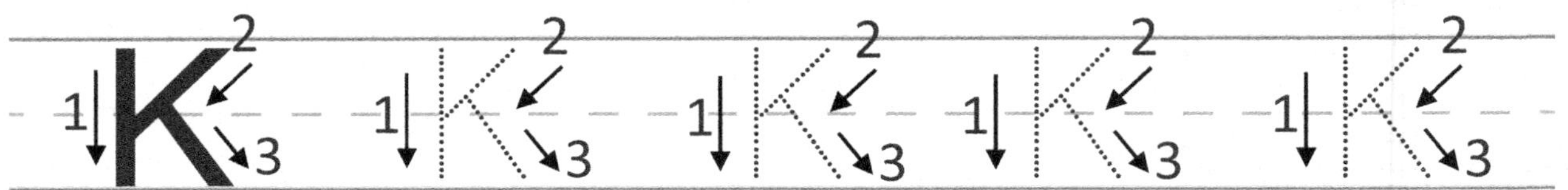
1 K 2 3
1 K 2 3
1 K 2 3
1 K 2 3
1 K 2 3

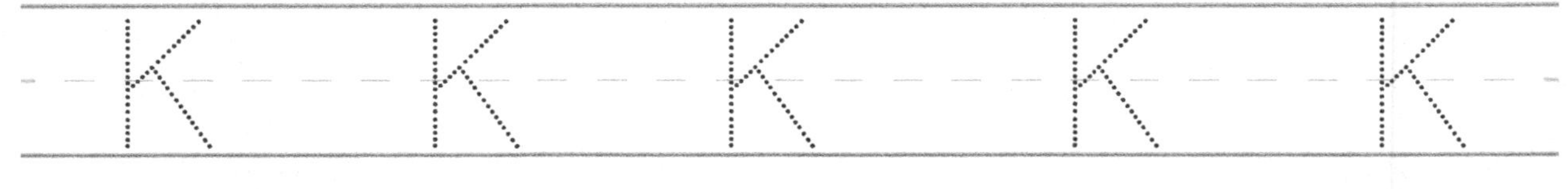
K K K K K

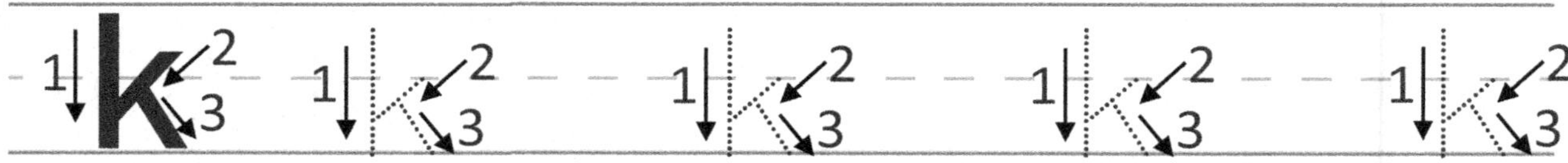
1 k 2 3
1 k 2 3
1 k 2 3
1 k 2 3
1 k 2 3

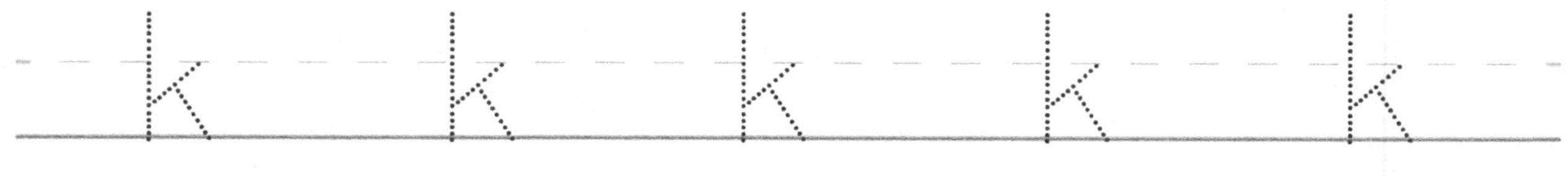
k k k k k

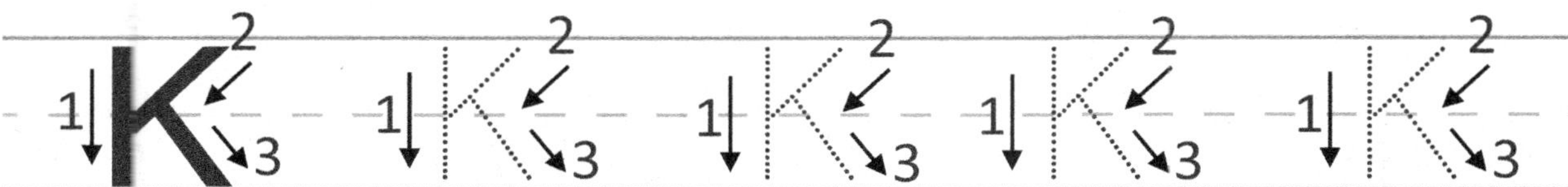

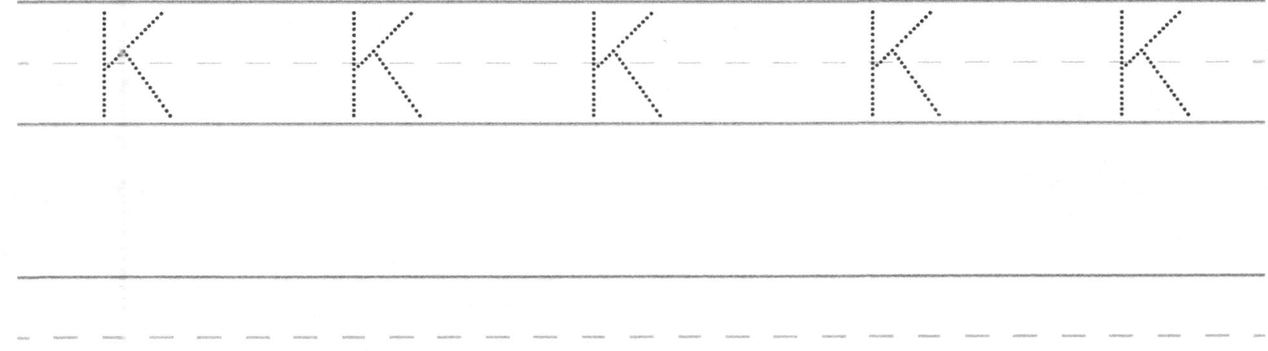

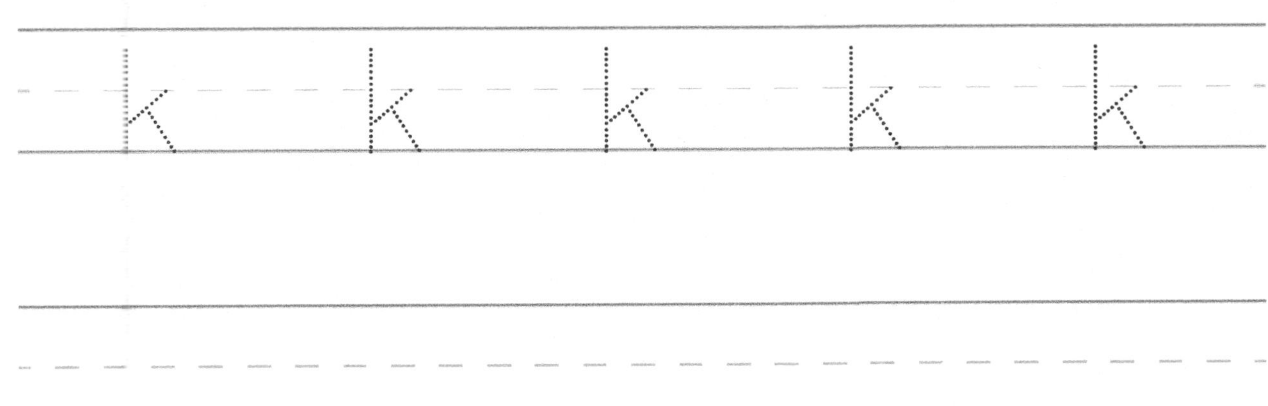

Kobe Bryant

Pro Basketball Player

Ketanji Brown Jackson

1st Black Female Supreme Court Justice

King Jaffe Joffer

King of Zamunda "Coming to America"

Kamala Harris

1st Female Vice President

Kangol

Kirk Franklin

Choir Director, Singer, Songwriter

Kwanzaa

Cultural Holiday Celebration

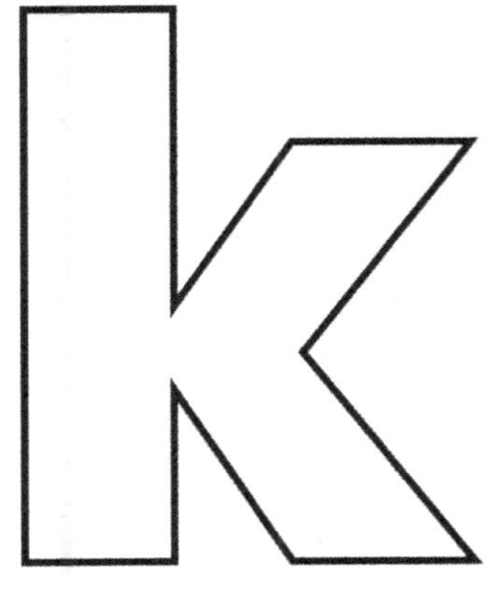

Kaepernick

Colin Kaepernick
Freedom Fighter, Pro Football Player

1 L 2 → 1 L 2 → 1 L 2 → 1 L 2 → 1 L 2 →

L L L L L

1 l l l l l

l l l l l

1 L 2 → 1 L 2 → 1 L 2 → 1 L 2 → 1 L 2 →

1 l

Lawrence Taylor
Hall of Fame Pro Football Player
Lawnmower
Invented by John A. Burr
Ludacris
Rapper, Actor, Record Label Owner
Liberia
Country in Africa
L

Louis Armstrong

Influential Jazz Trumpeter

Lipgloss

Locs

Lisa Leslie

Pro Basketball Player, Sports Analyst

Lisa 'Left Eye' Lopes

Rapper, Singer

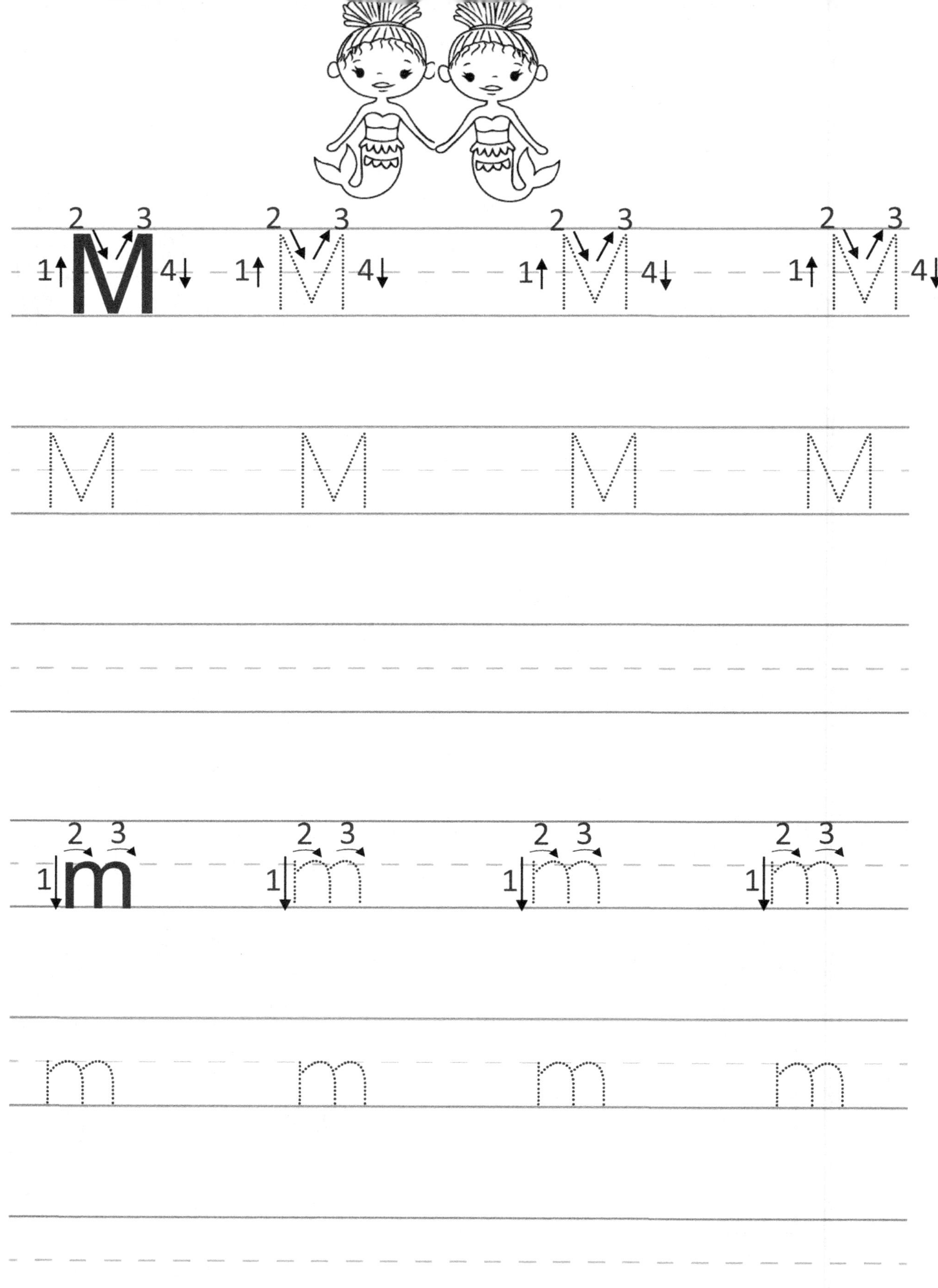

2 3
1 M 4
2 3
1 M 4
2 3
1 M 4
2 3
1 M 4
M M M M
2 3
1 m
2 3
1 m
2 3
1 m
2 3
1 m
m m m m

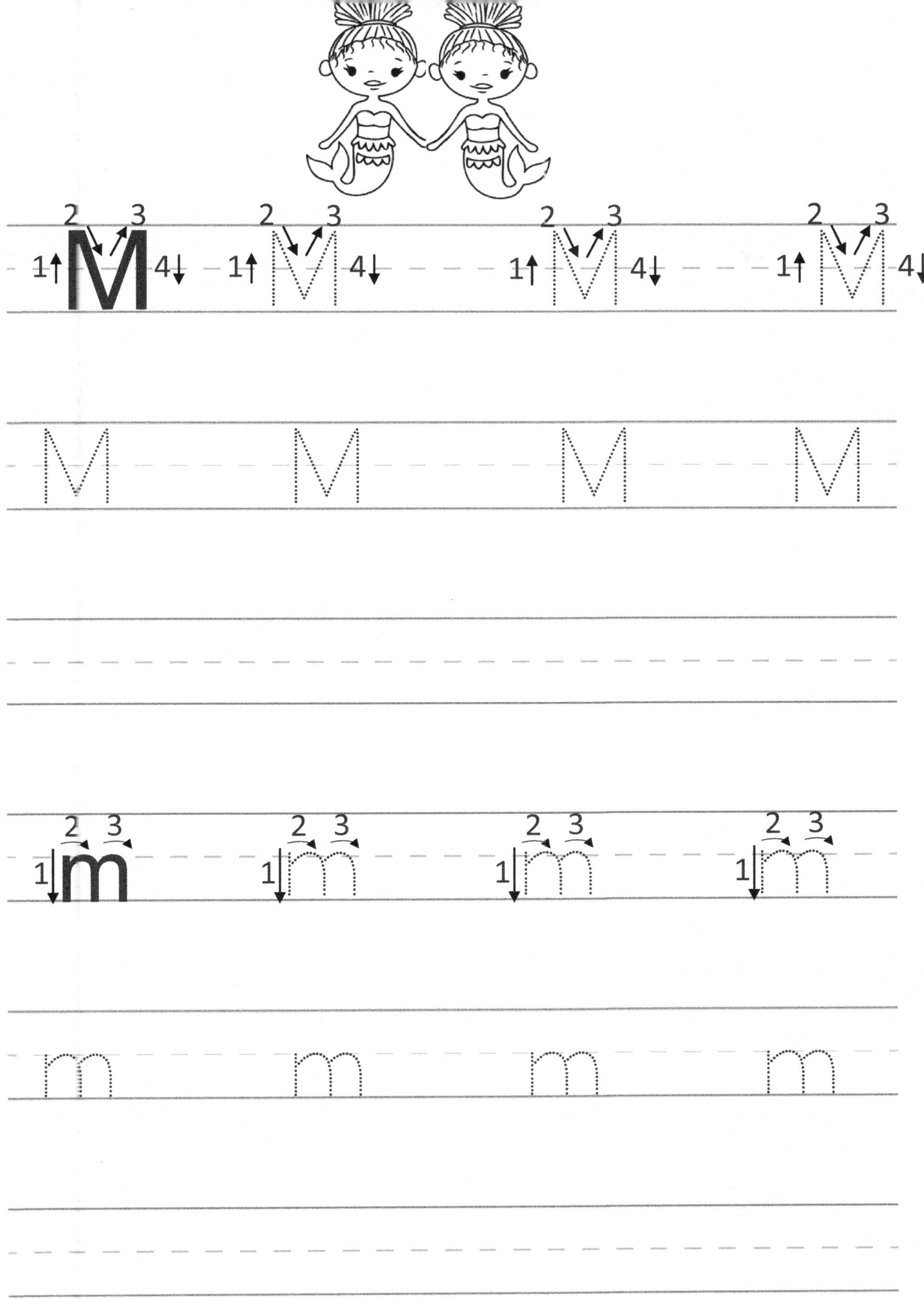
2 3
1 M 4
m
2 3
1 m

Majorette

Mary J. Blige

Singer, Songwriter, Actress

Marsai Martin

Actress

Madame C.J. Walker

1st Female Self-made Millionaire

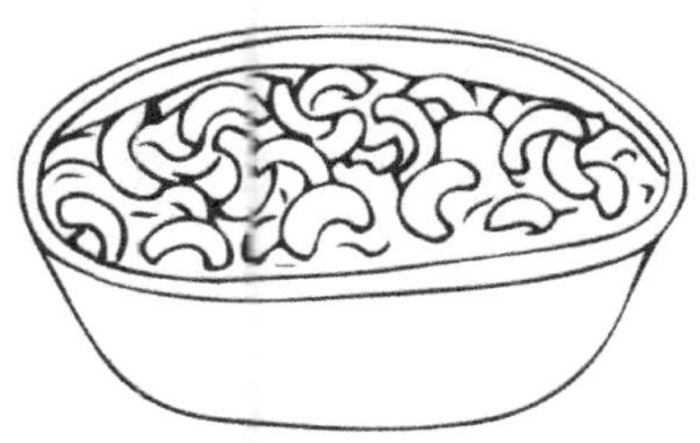

Macaroni & Cheese

Motown

Record Label

Maxine Waters

House of Congress Representative

Mansa Musa

King of Mali Empire, Richest Man to Ever Live

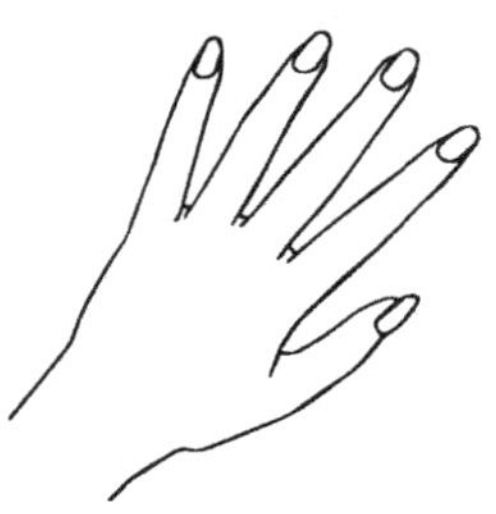

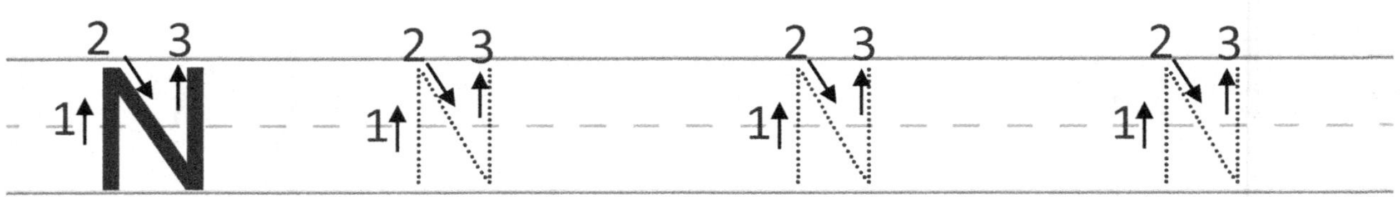
2 3
1 N

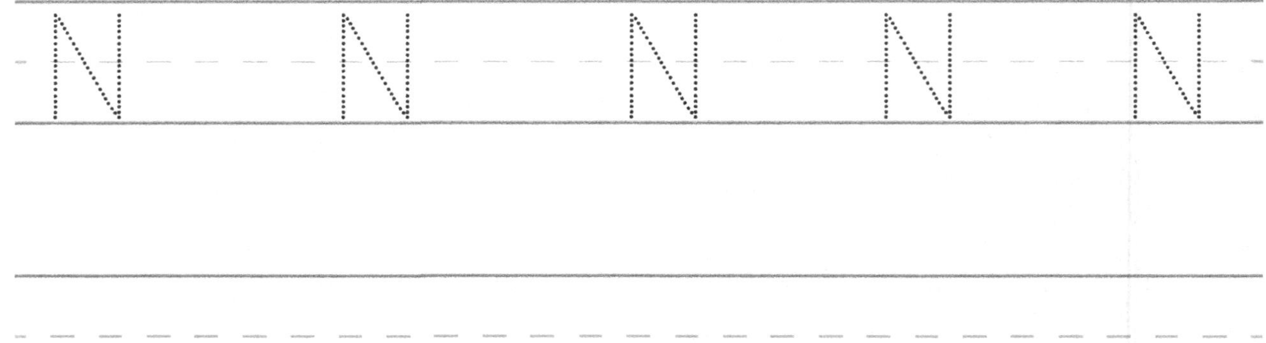

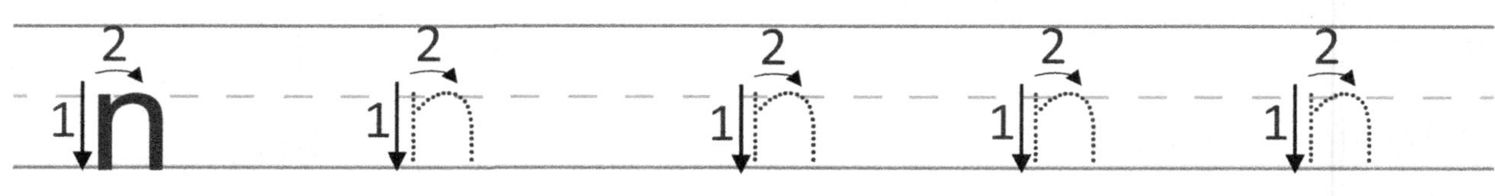
2
1 n

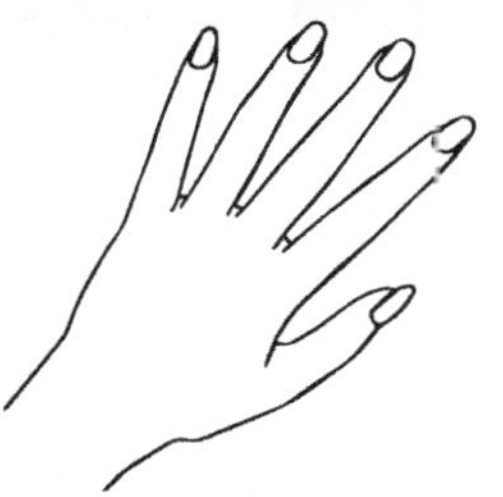

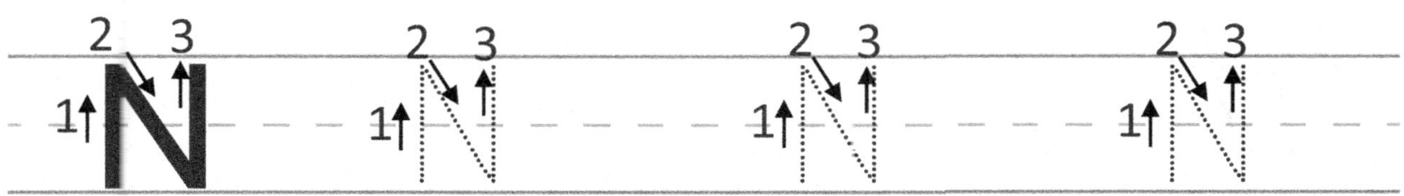

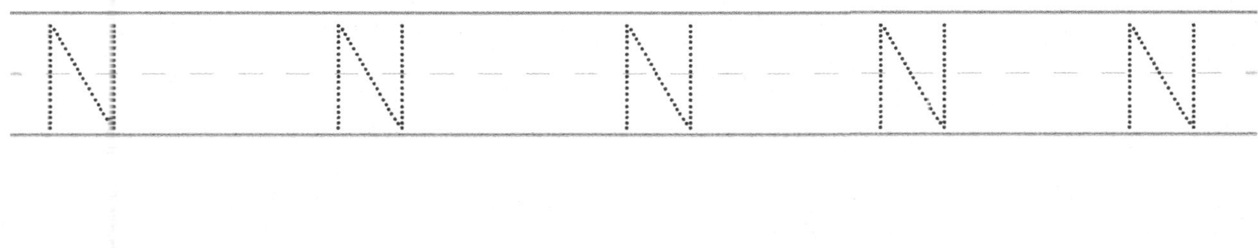

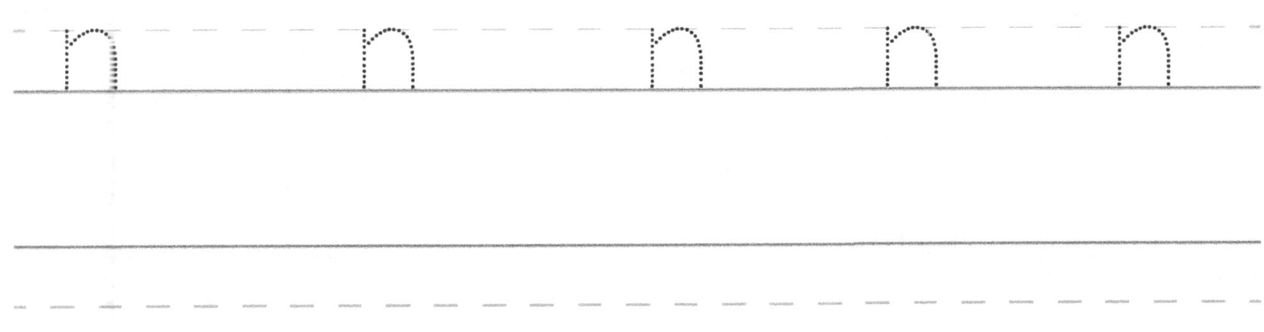

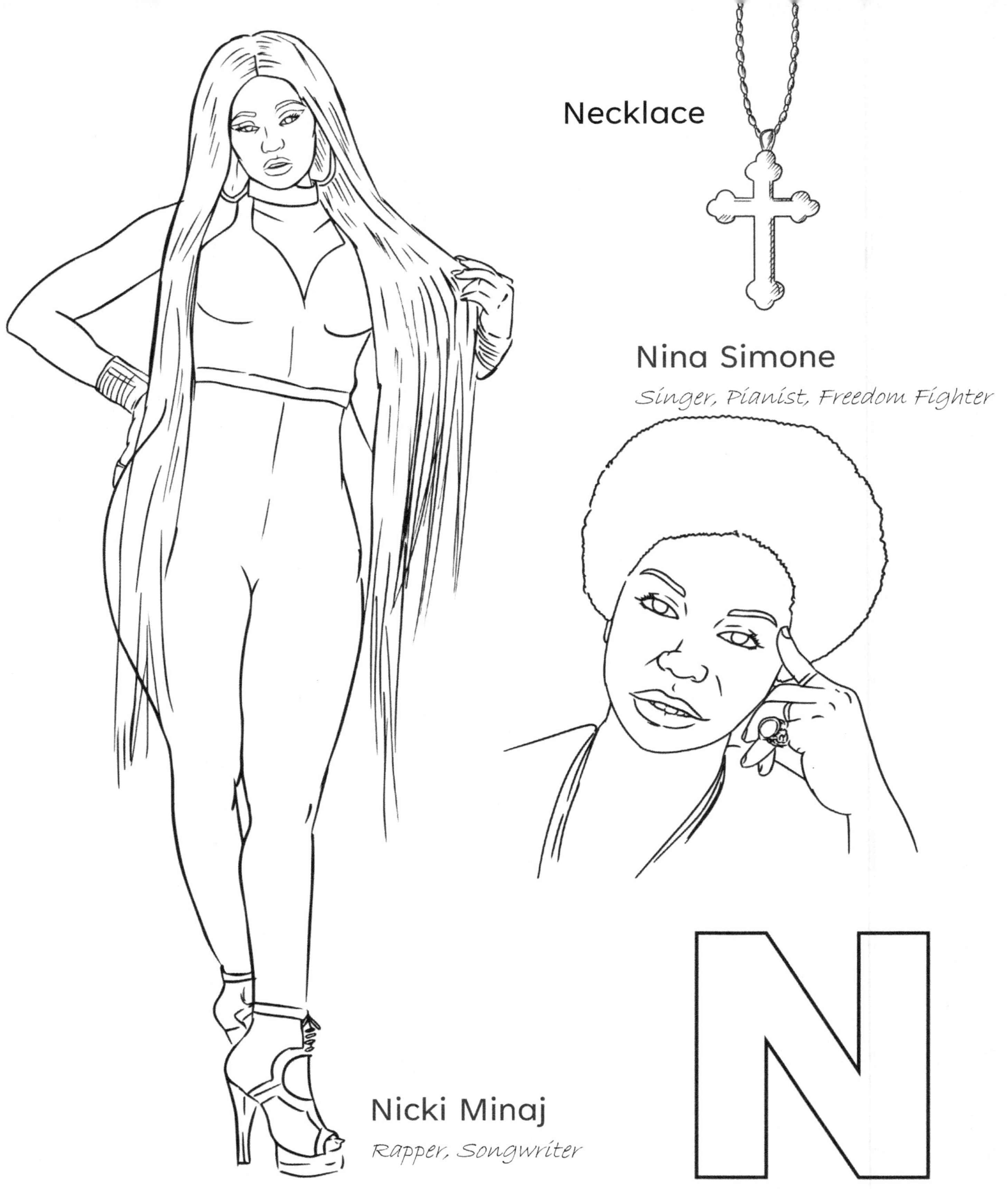
Necklace
Nina Simone
Singer, Pianist, Freedom Fighter
N
Nicki Minaj
Rapper, Songwriter

Nigeria
Country in Africa
Noodles
Nas
Rapper, Actor
n
Nelson Mandela
Pres. Of South Africa, Freedom Fighter

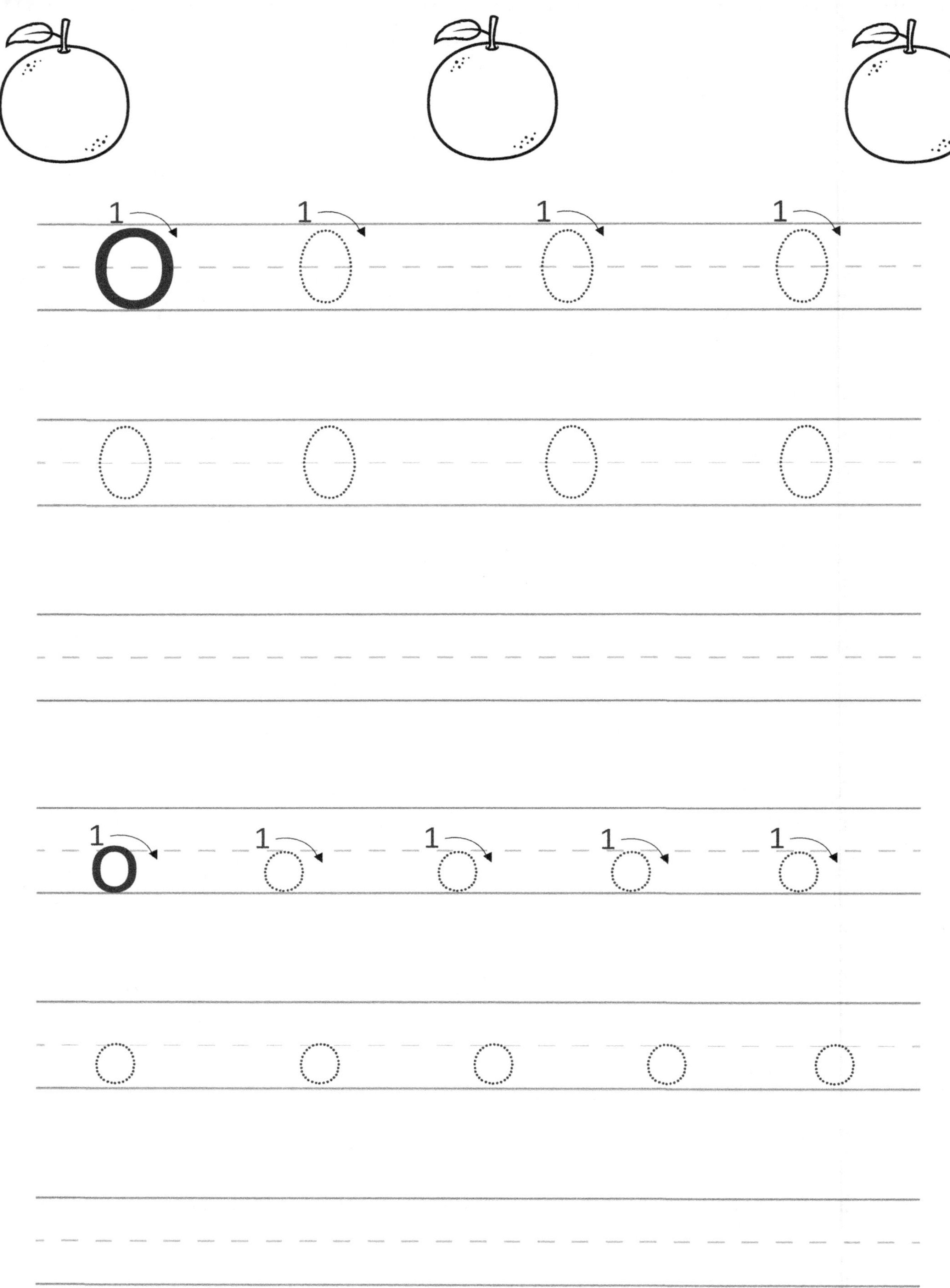
1
O
1
1
1
1
o
1
1
1
1

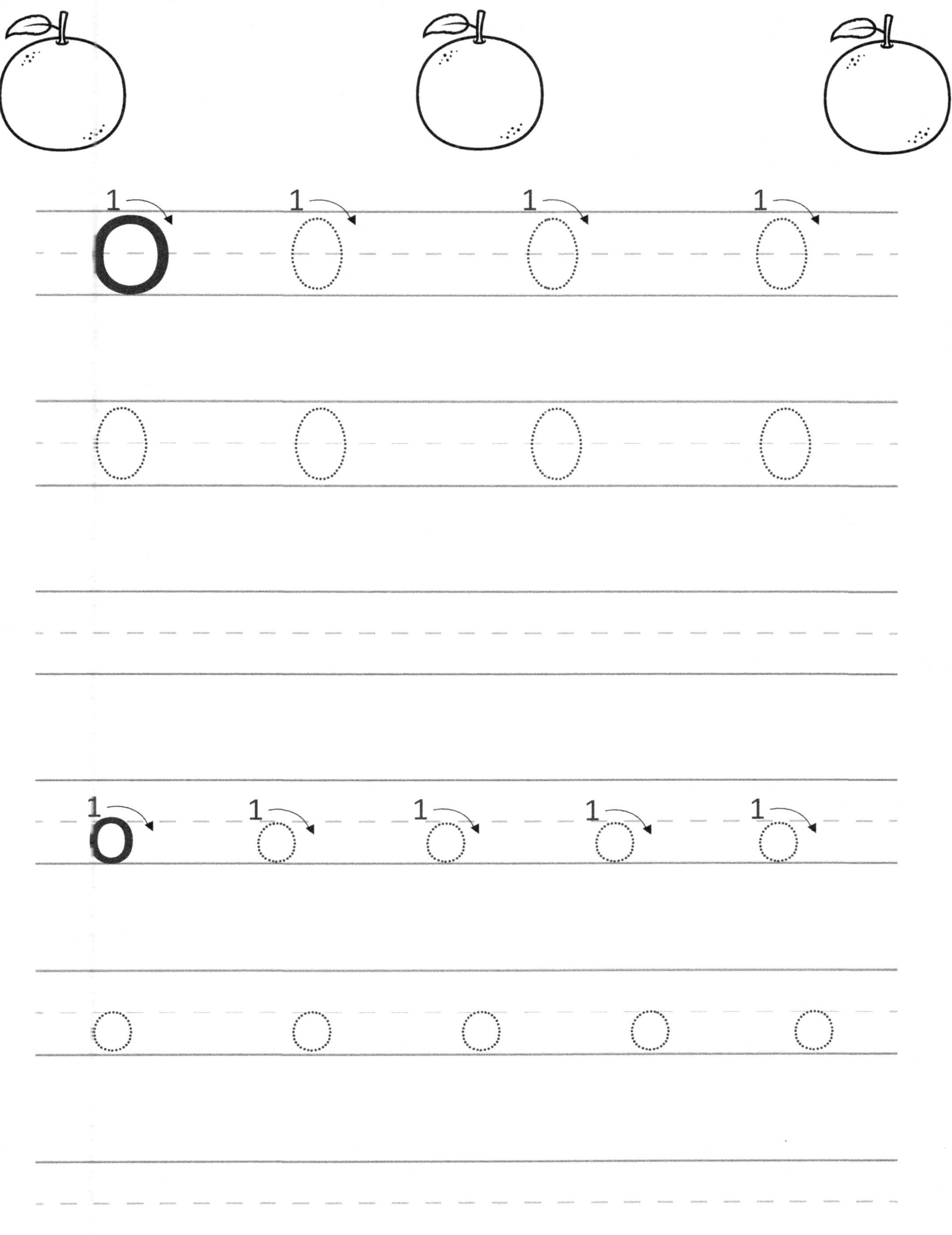

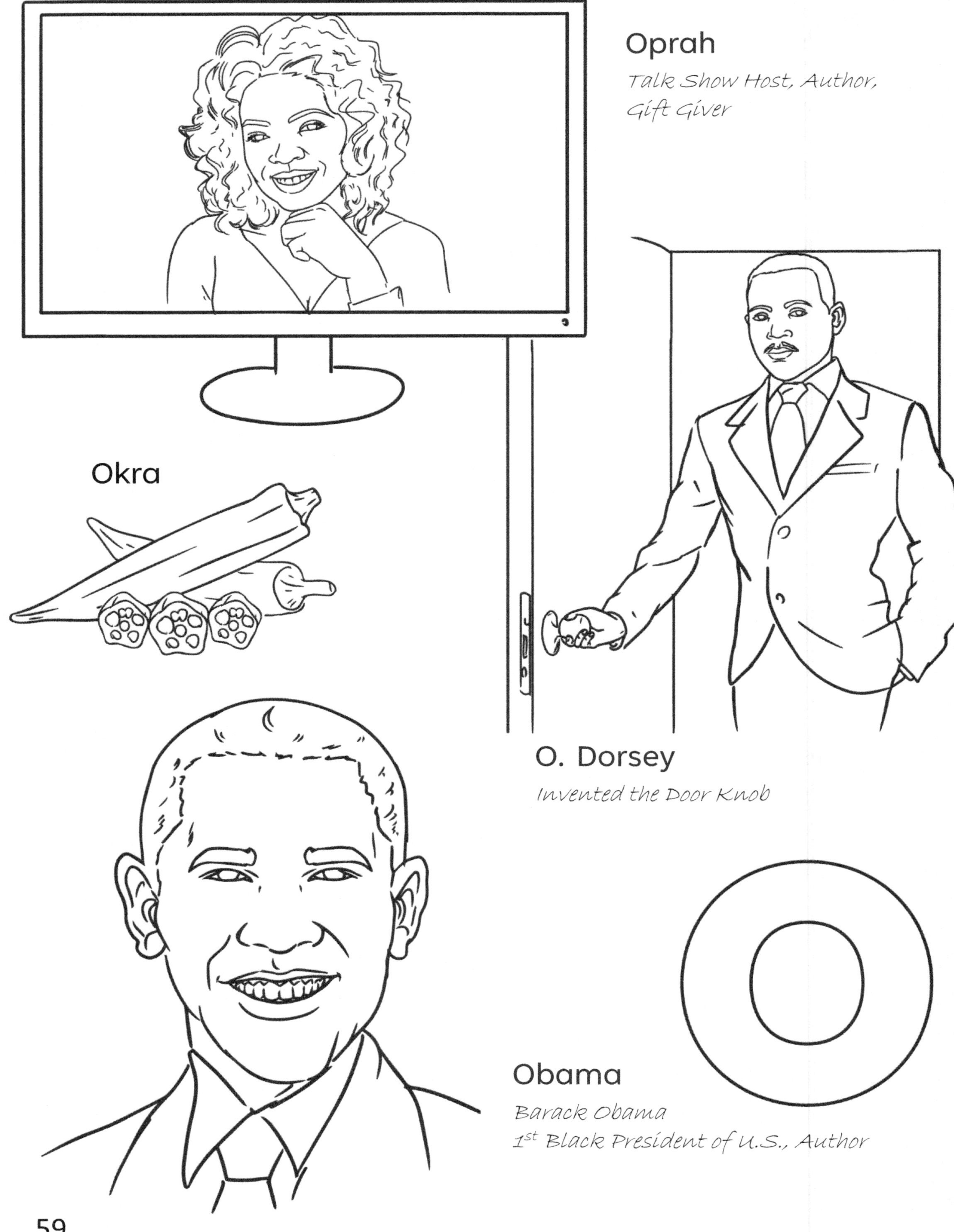
Oprah
Talk Show Host, Author,
Gift Giver
Okra
O. Dorsey
Invented the Door Knob
Obama
Barack Obama
1st Black President of U.S., Author
O

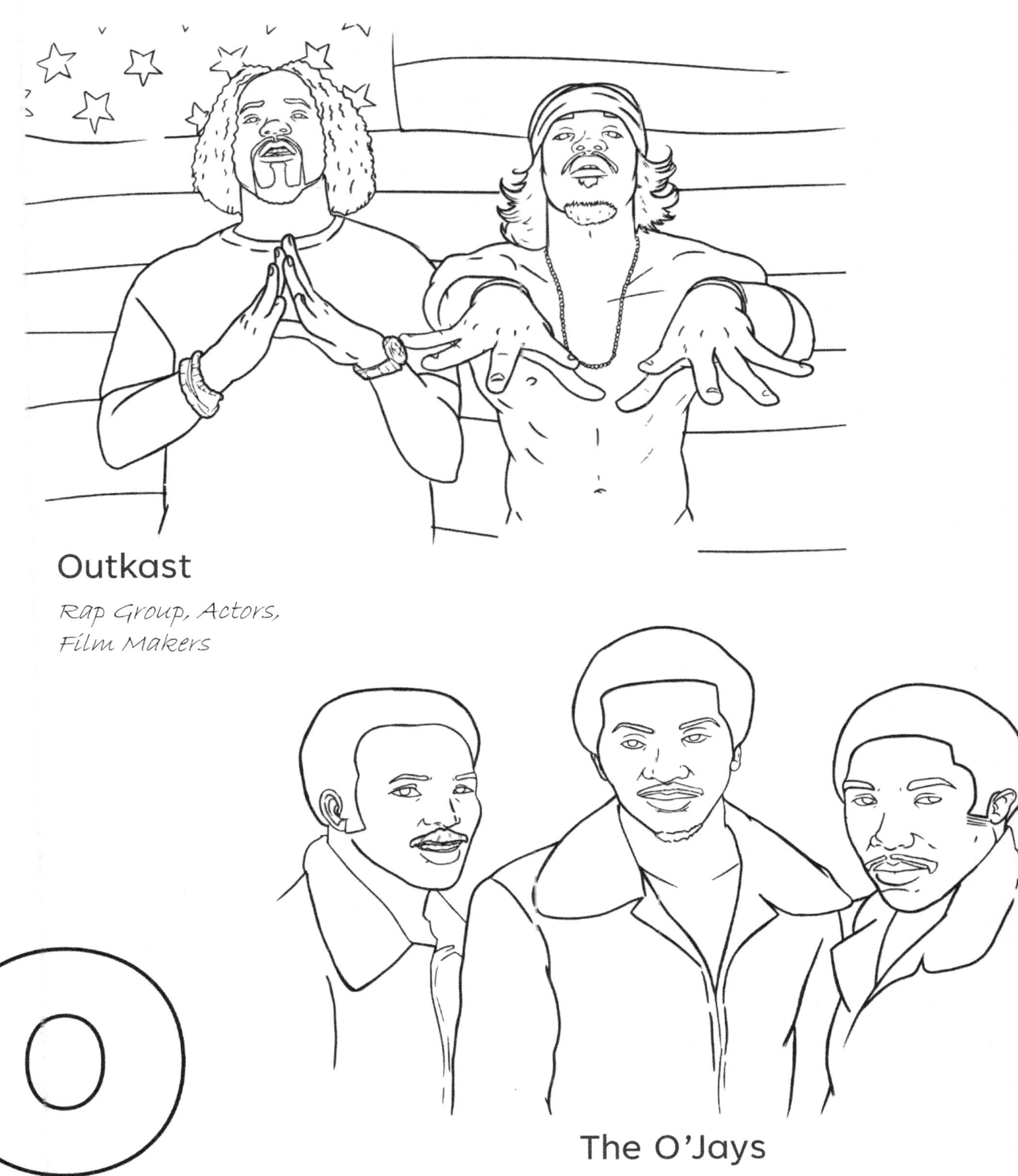

Outkast

Rap Group, Actors, Film Makers

The O'Jays

R&B Group

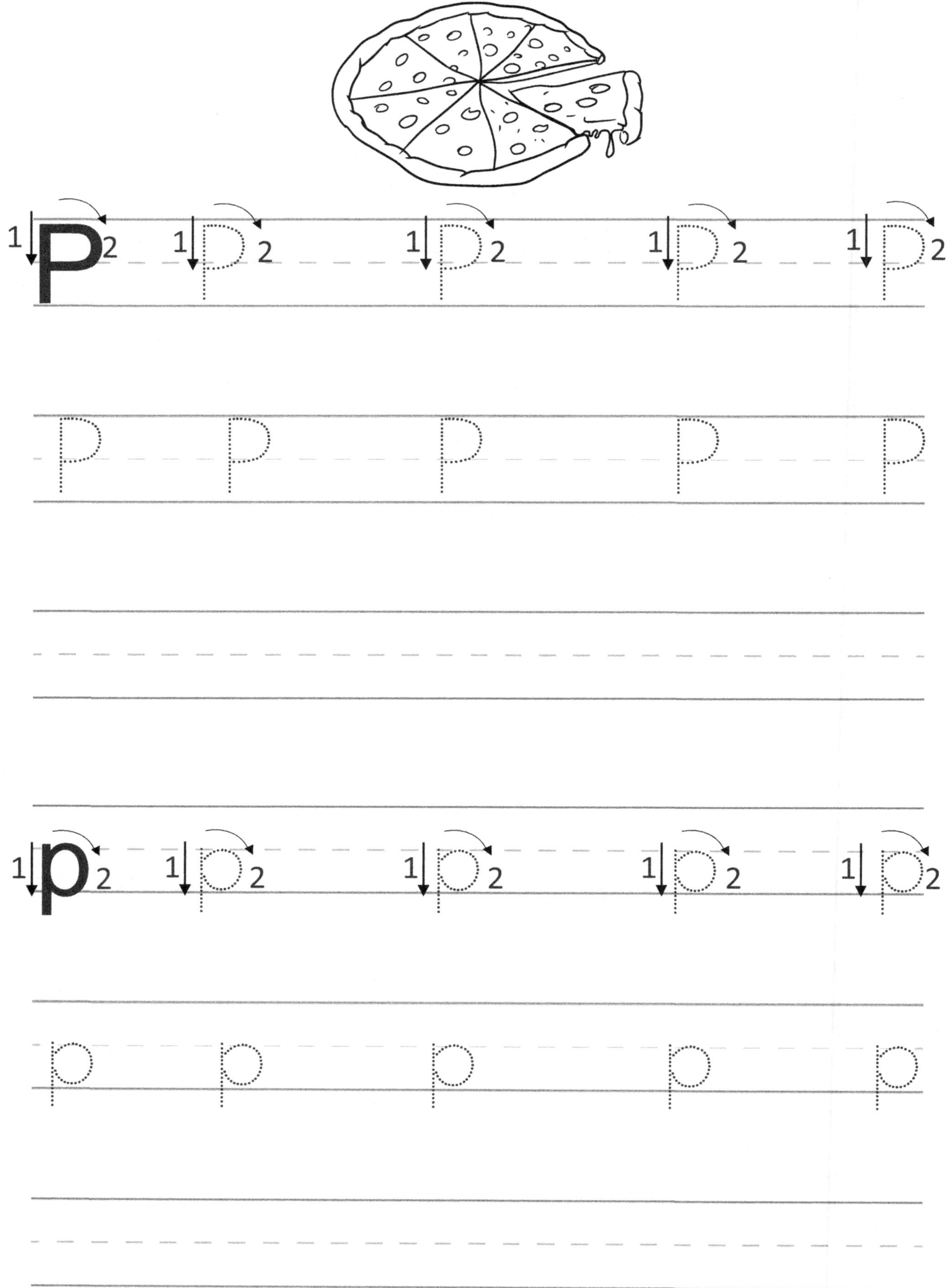

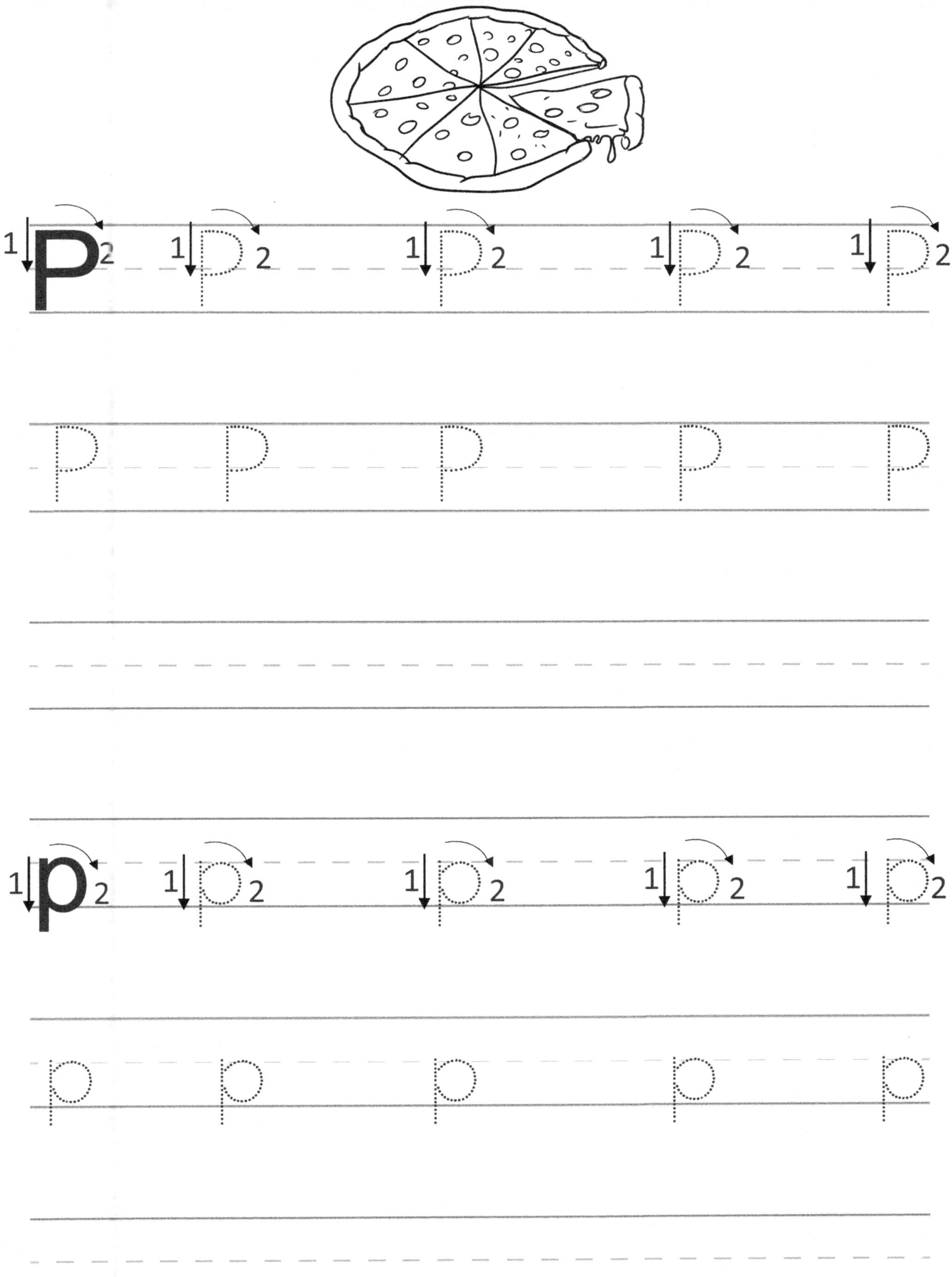

Paul Robeson
Concert Artist, Actor,
Pro Football Player
Prince
Singer, Songwriter, Gift Giver
Peanuts
Pecan Pie
P

Peace Sign

Phylicia Rashad

Actress. Director, Dean at Howard Univ.

p

Patti LaBelle

Singer, Actress, Businesswoman

UNITED STATES OF AMERICA
IN GOD WE TRUST
LIBERTY
QUARTER DOLLAR

1 Q 2

q 2

UNITED STATES OF AMERICA
IN GOD WE TRUST
LIBERTY
QUARTER DOLLAR

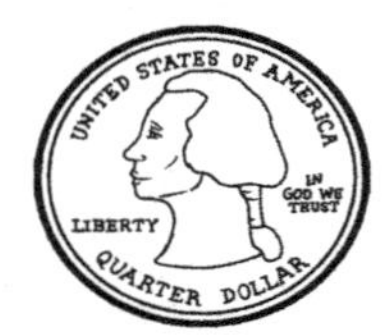

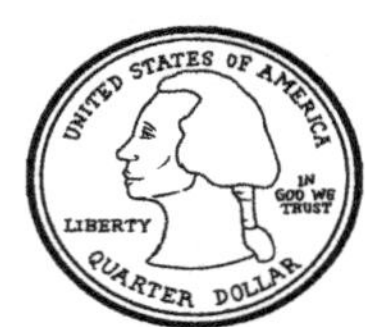

1 Q 2 1 Q 2 1 Q 2 1 Q 2 1 Q 2

Q Q Q Q Q

1 q 2 1 q 2 1 q 2 1 q 2 1 q 2

q q q q q

Quavo

Rapper

Questlove

Pro Drummer, Music Reporter

Quincy Jones

Producer, Composer, Arranger

Quartet

Group of 4 Singers

q

Queen Ramonda

Queen of Wakanda "Black Panther"

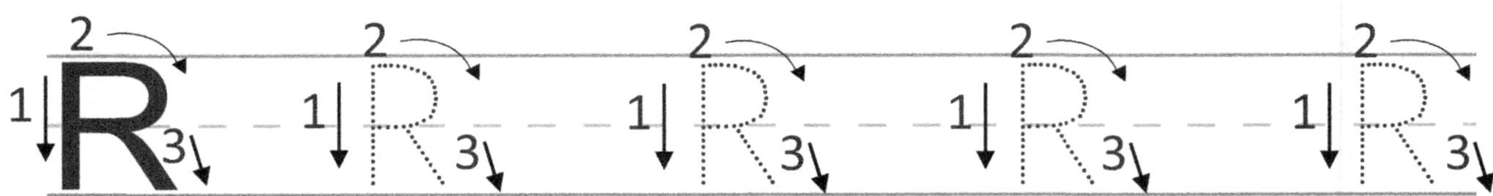

R R R R R

r r r r r

r r r r r

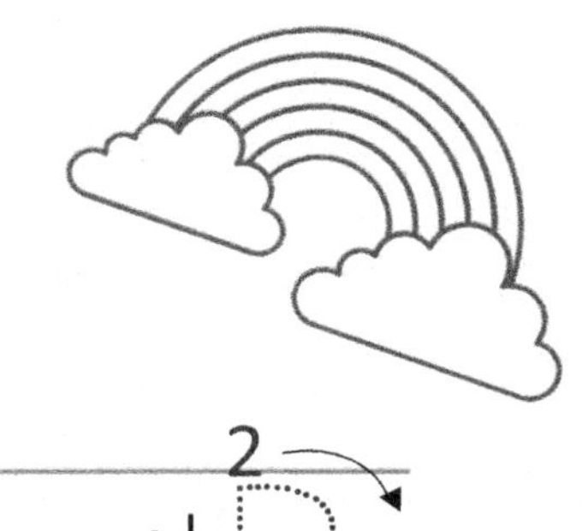

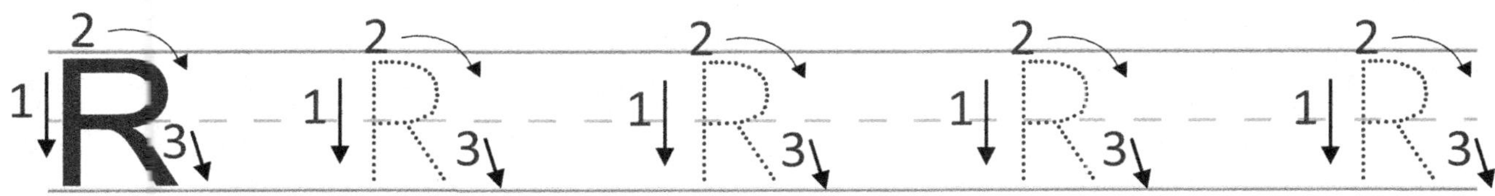

2 1 r 2 1 r 2 1 r 2 1 r 2 1 r

r r r r r

Rims

Rihanna

Singer, Fashion Icon, Business Owner

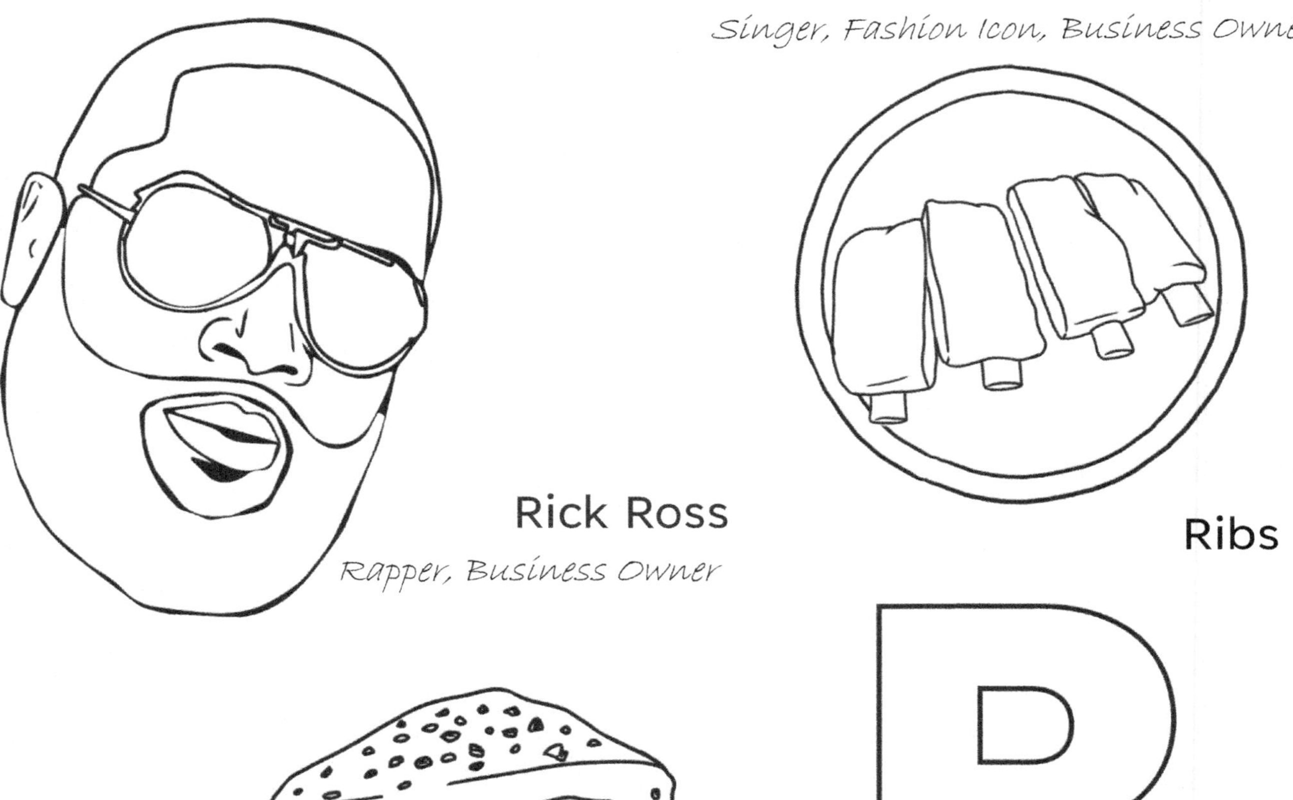

Rick Ross

Rapper, Business Owner

Ribs

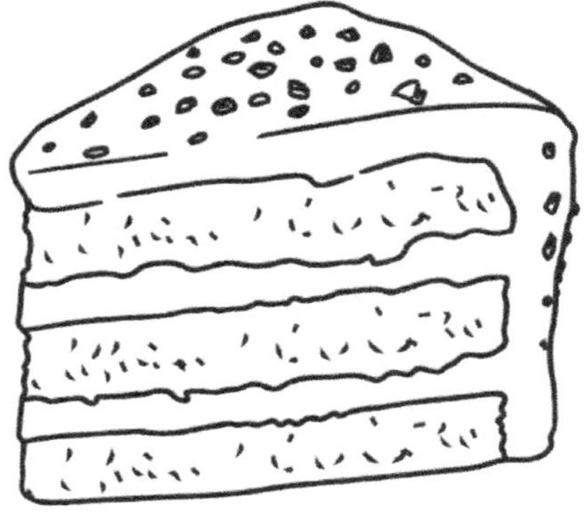

Red Velvet Cake

Run-D.M.C.

Hip-hop Group

Ralph Bunche

Nobel Peace Prize Winner, Diplomat

Randy Moss

Pro Football Player

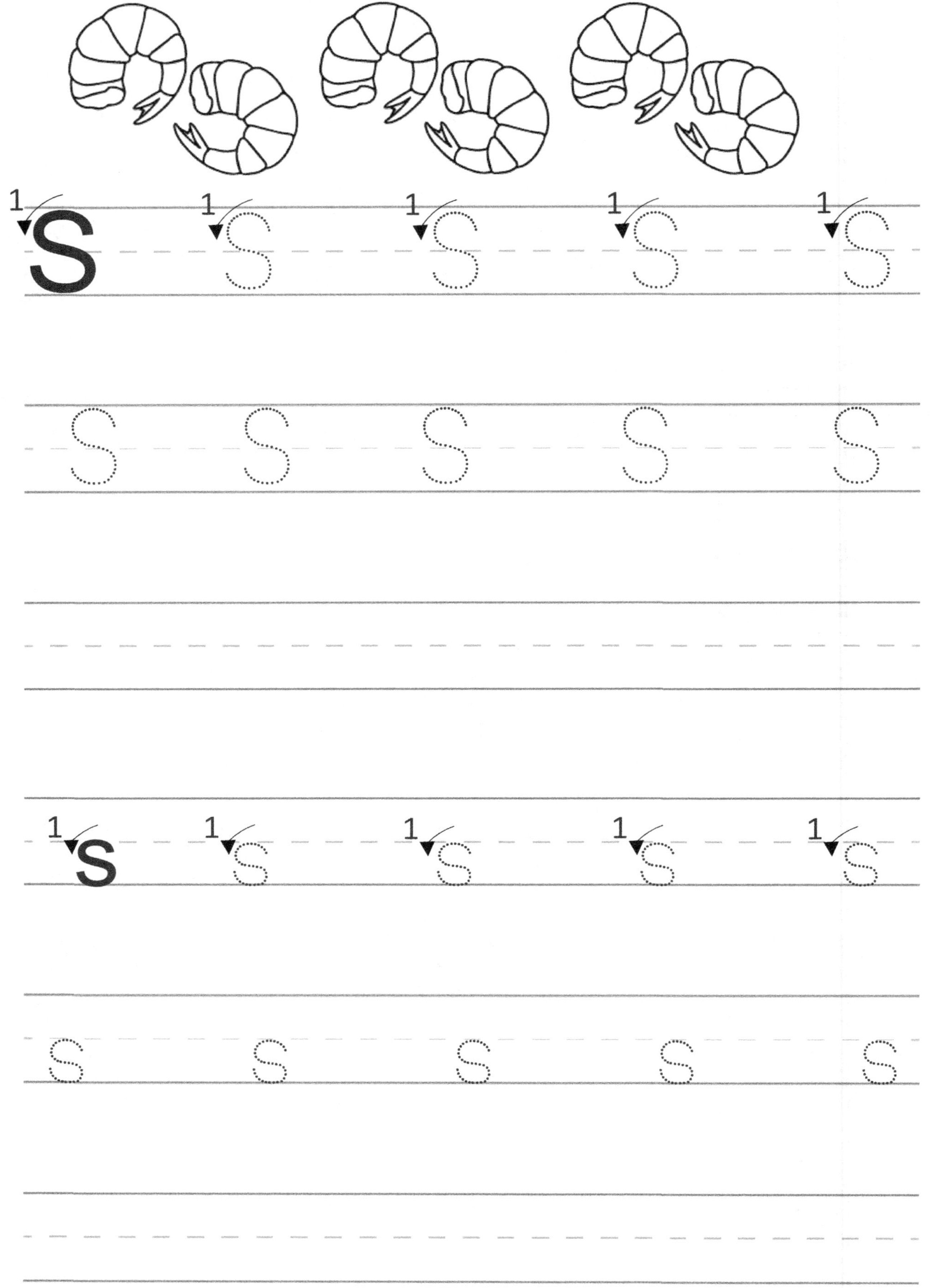
1 S 1 S 1 S 1 S 1 S
S S S S S
1 s 1 s 1 s 1 s 1 s
s s s s s

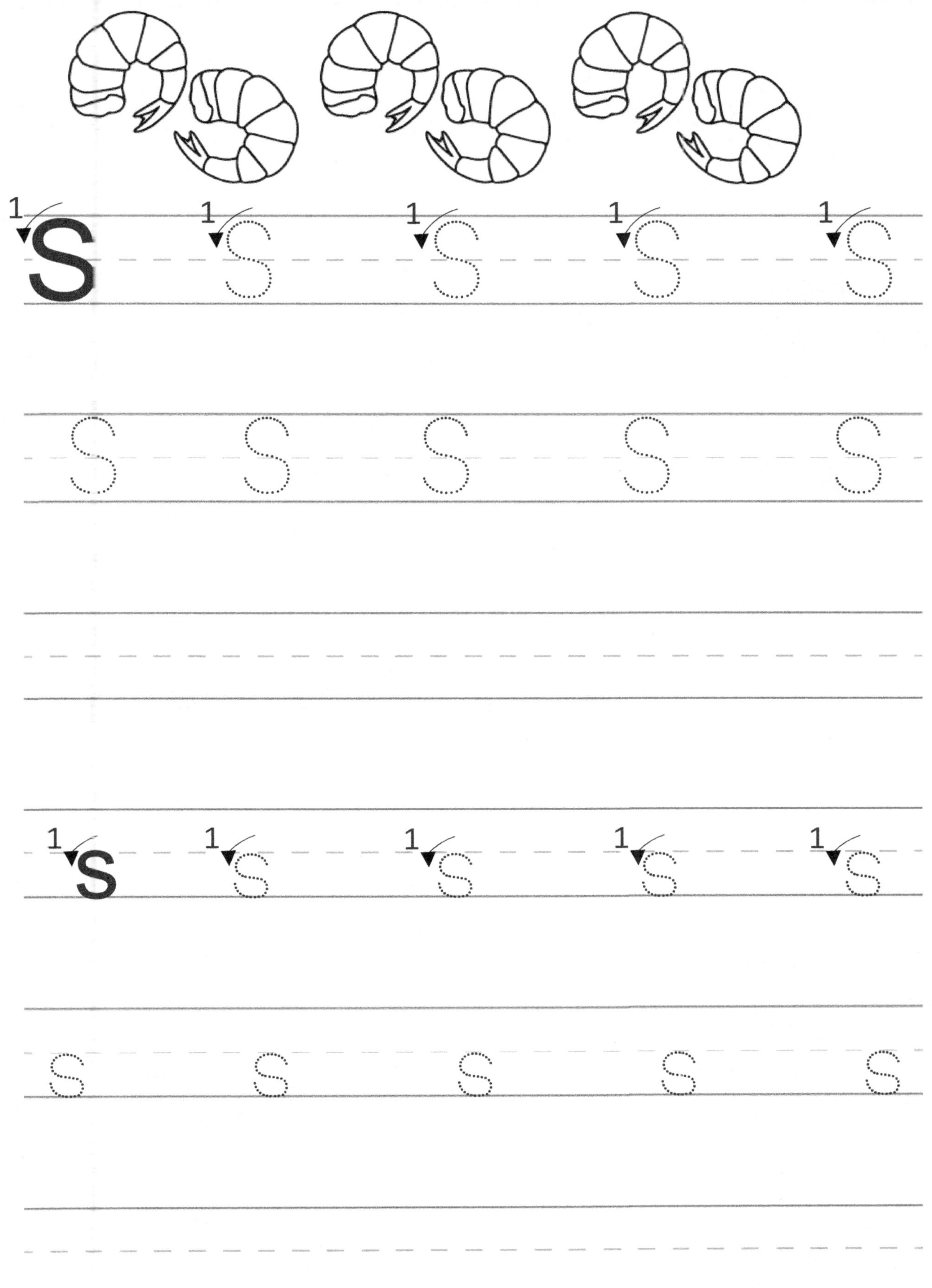
S
s

Sneaker
Sidney Poitier
Actor, Film Director, Diplomat
Spades
Step Team
SOUL
TRAIN
Soul Train TV Show
Celebrated Black Culture
S

Snoop Dogg

Rapper, Actor. Business Owner

Second Line

New Orleans
Parade Celebration

Super Soaker

Invented by Lonnie Johnson

Sojourner Truth

Freedom Fighter, Women's Rights Activist

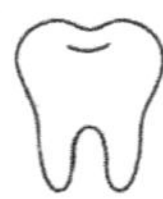
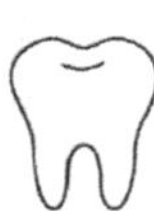

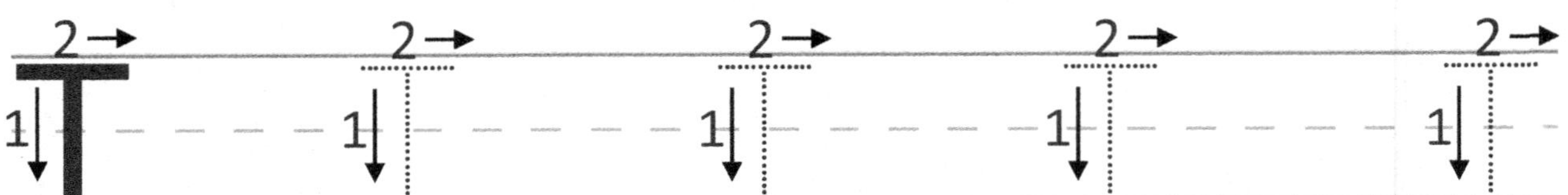

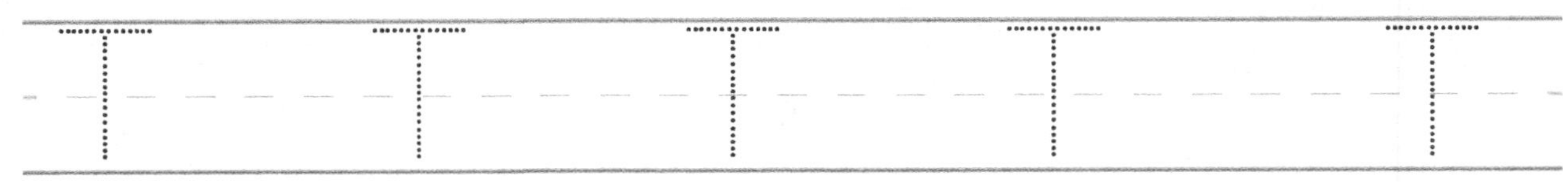

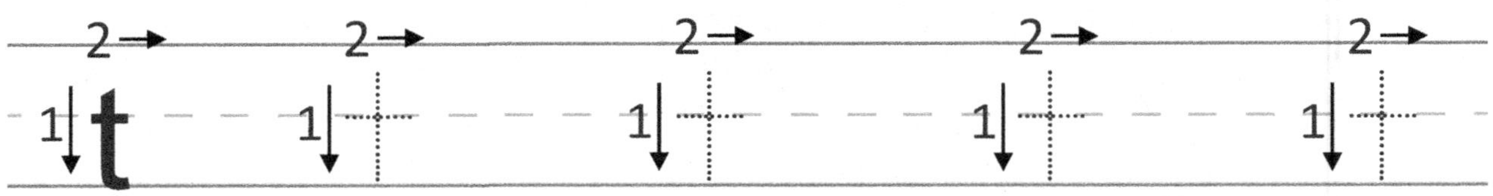

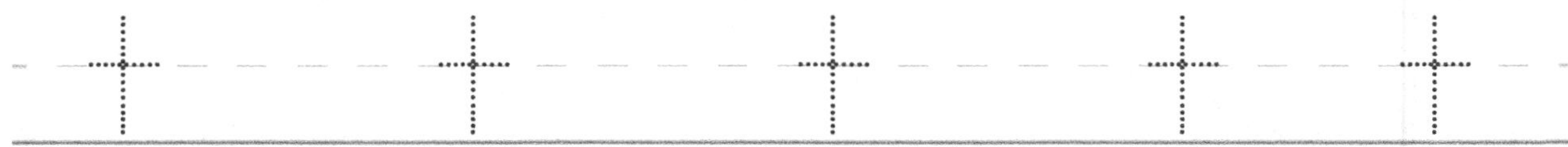

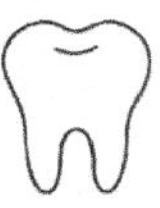
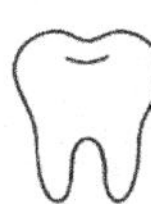
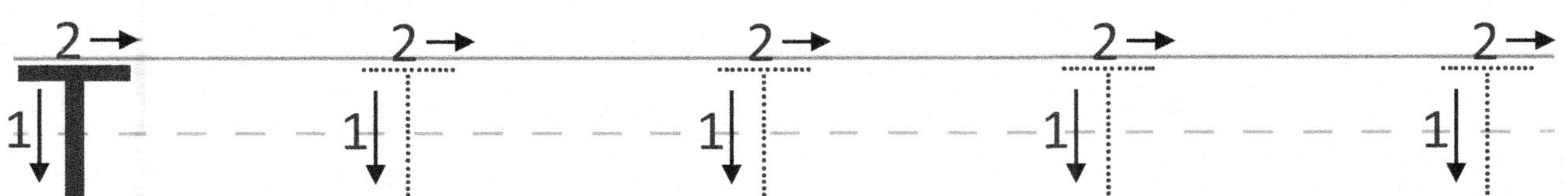
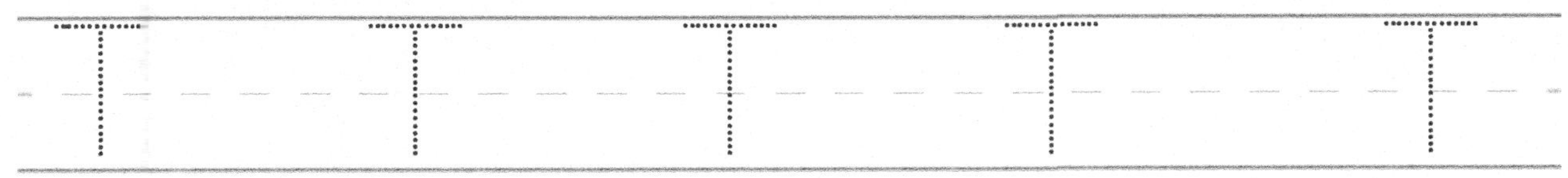
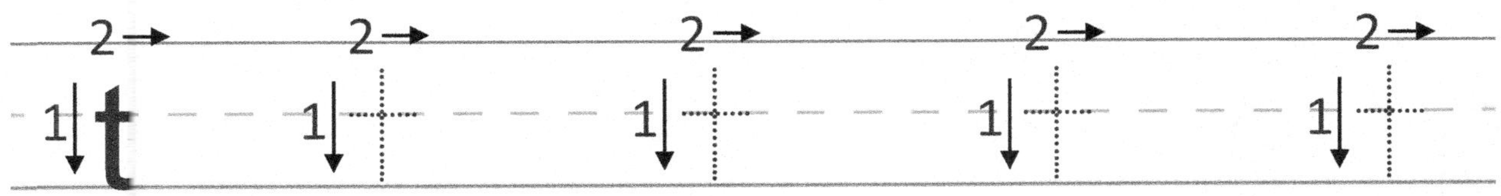
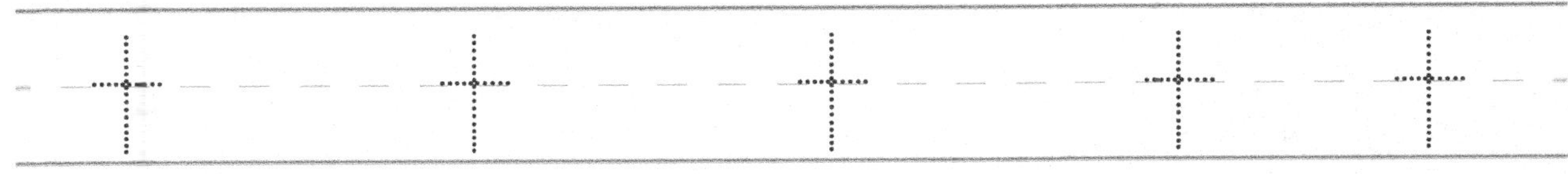
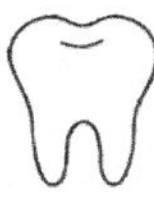

Tuskegee Airmen
Black Military Pilots of WWII
Tina Turner
Queen of Rock 'n Roll
Twists
Toussaint Louverture
Haitian Freedom Fighter
T

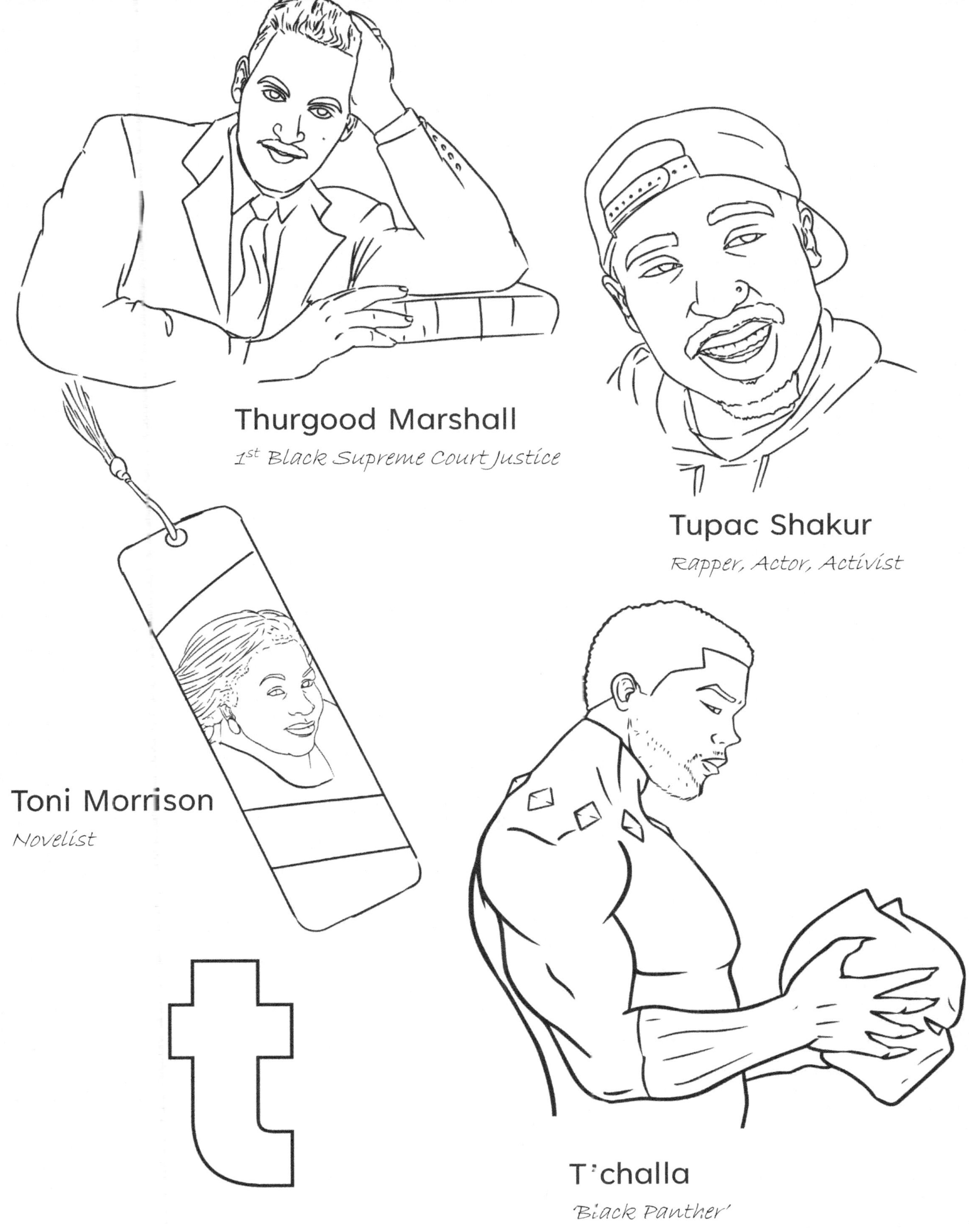
Thurgood Marshall
1st Black Supreme Court Justice
Tupac Shakur
Rapper, Actor, Activist
Toni Morrison
Novelist
t
T'challa
'Black Panther'

1 U 2 1 U 2 1 U 2 1 U 2 1 U 2

U U U U U

1 u 2 1 u 2 1 u 2 1 u 2 1 u 2

u u u u u

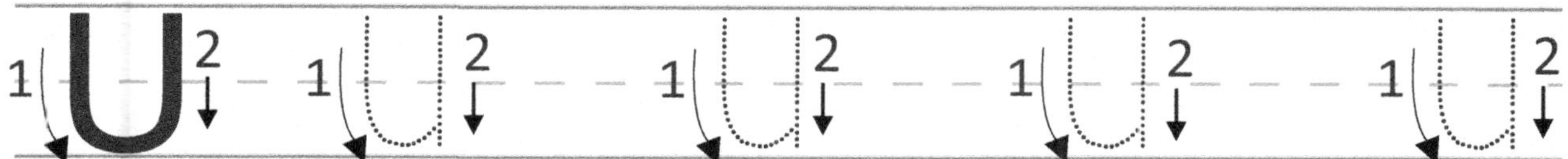

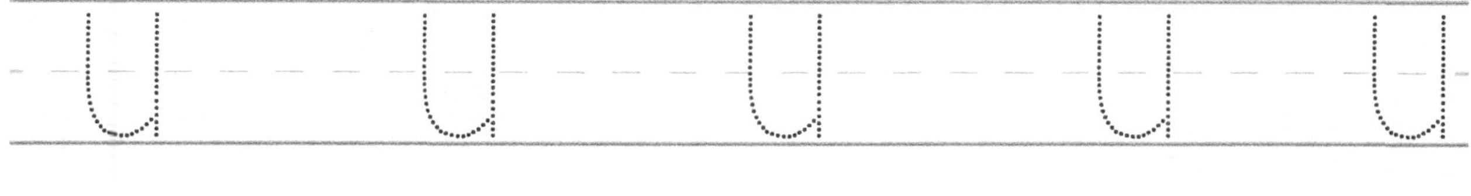

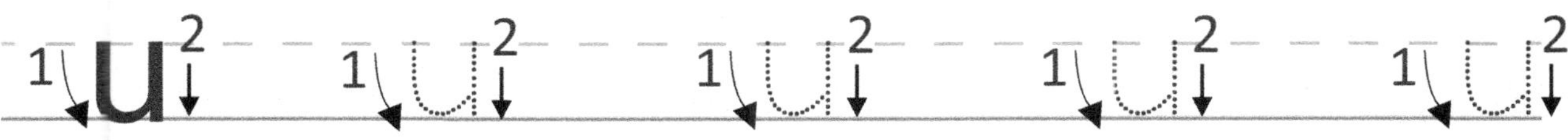

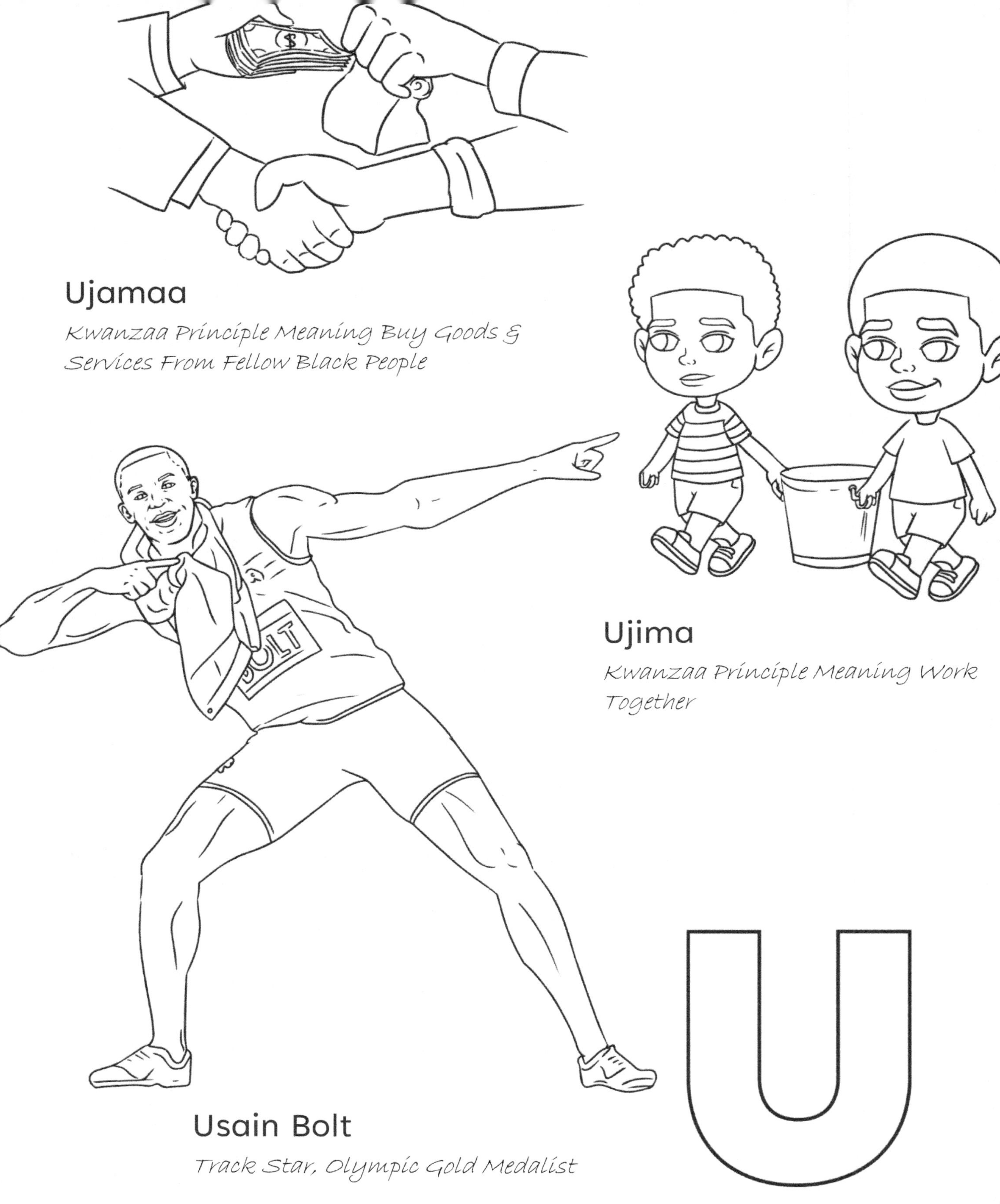

Ujamaa

Kwanzaa Principle Meaning Buy Goods & Services From Fellow Black People

Ujima

Kwanzaa Principle Meaning Work Together

Usain Bolt

Track Star, Olympic Gold Medalist

U

Uganda
Country in Africa
Uzo Aduba
Actress
Uncle Nearest
1st Black Master Distiller
u
Usher
R&B Singer

1 V 2 1 V 2 1 V 2 1 V 2 1 V 2

V V V V V

1 v 2 1 v 2 1 v 2 1 v 2 1 v 2

v v v v v

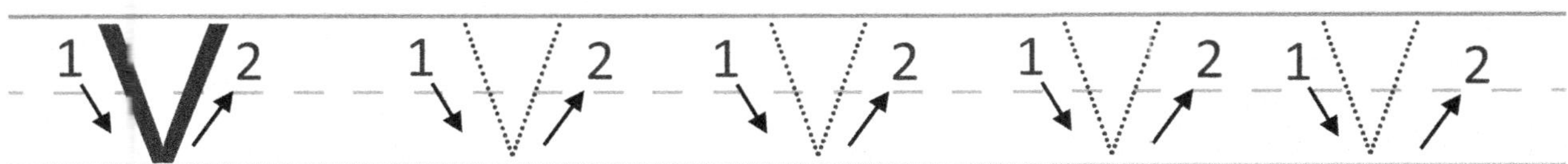

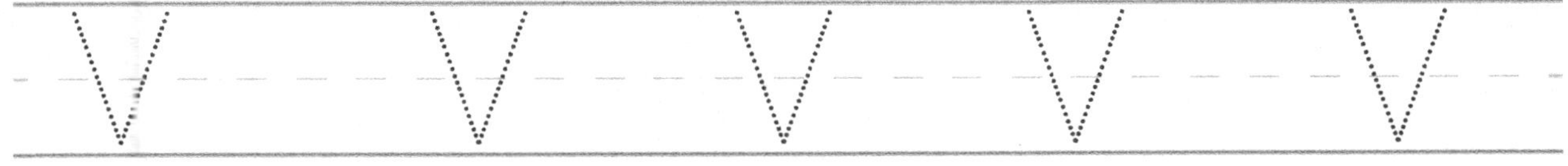

1 v 2 1 v 2 1 v 2 1 v 2 1 v 2

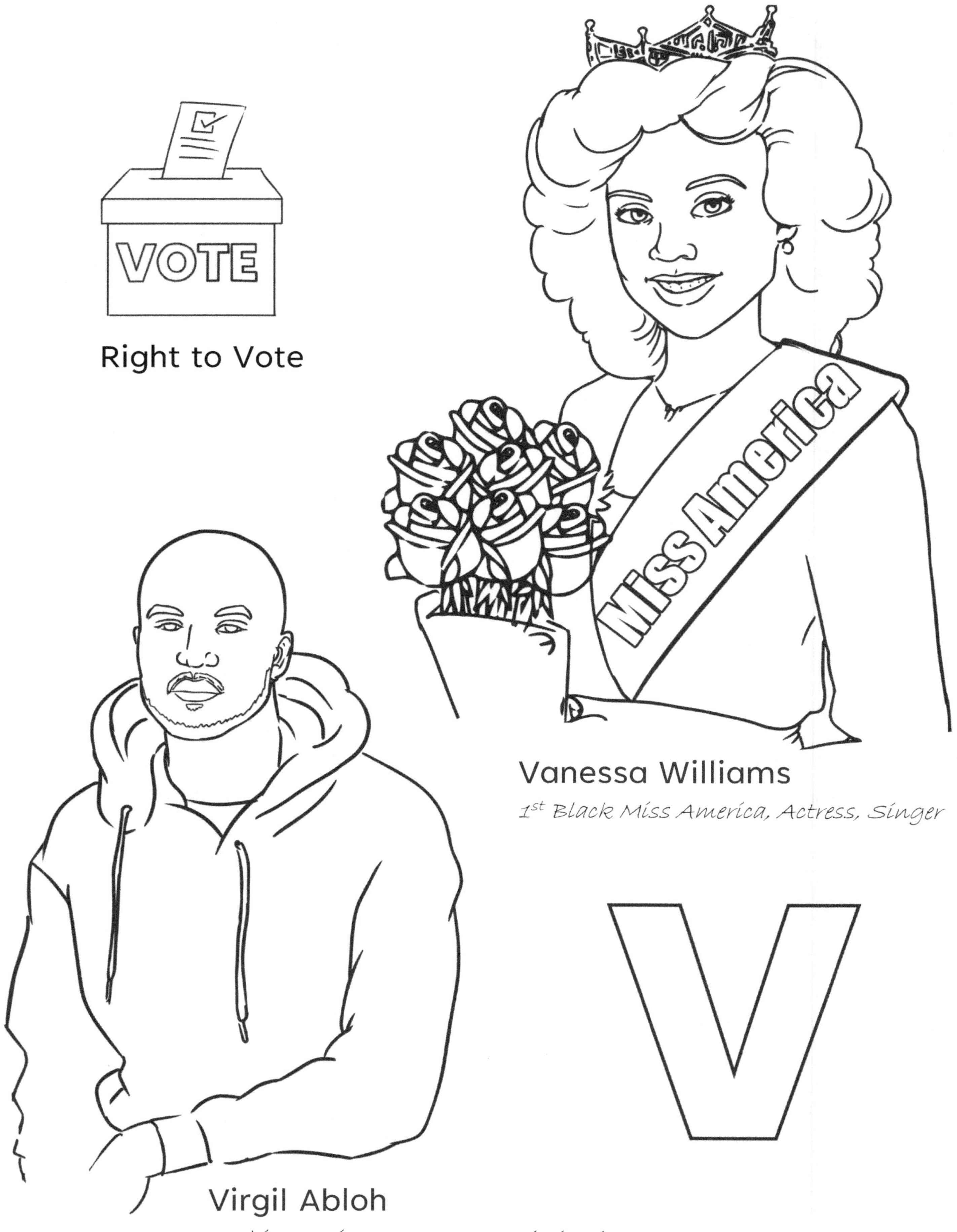

Right to Vote

Vanessa Williams

1st Black Miss America, Actress, Singer

Virgil Abloh

Fashion Designer, Luxury Artistic Director

Viola Davis

Award-winning Actress

Vivien Thomas

Heart Surgeon, Professor

Venus Williams

All-time Great Tennis Player

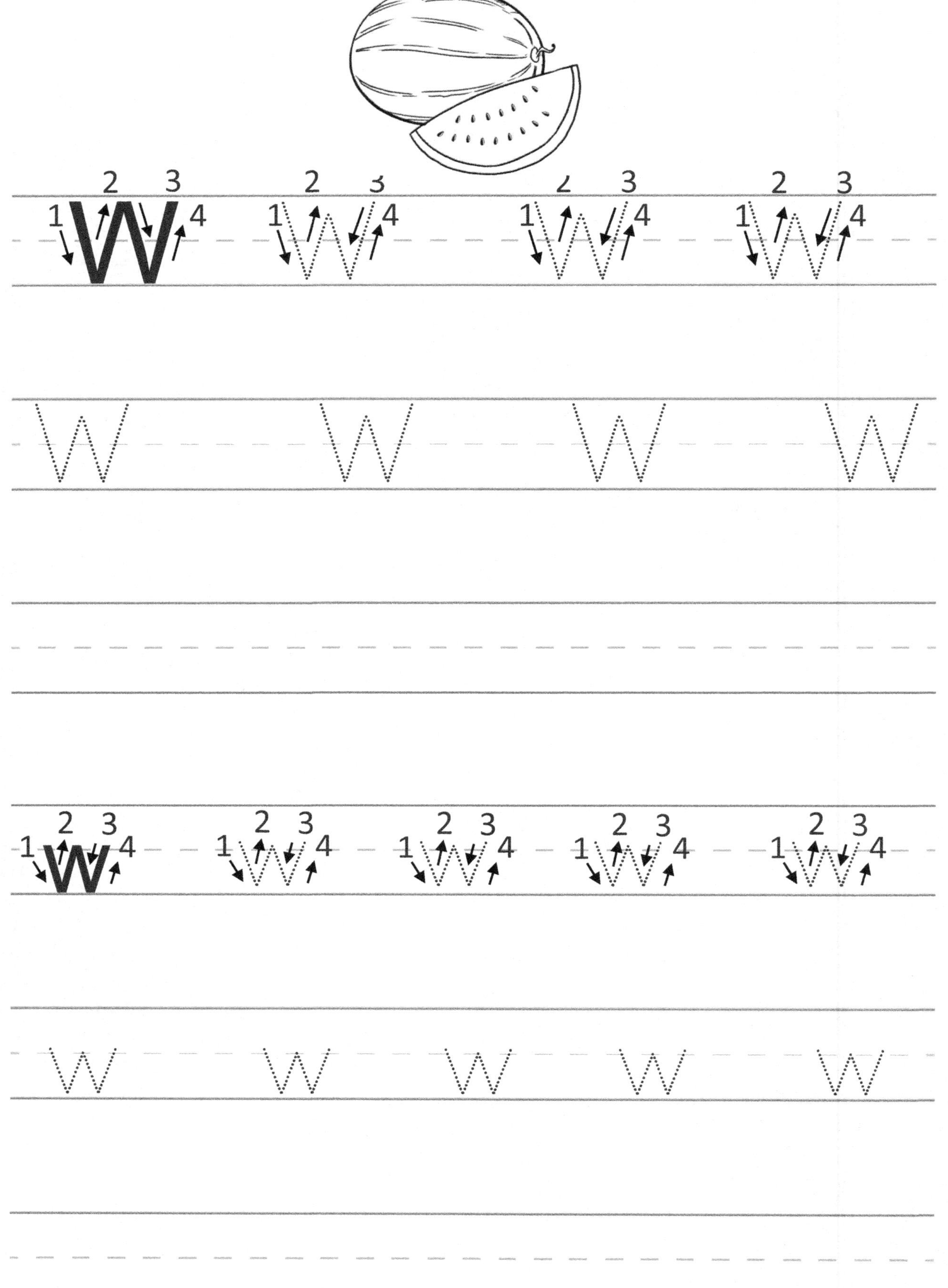

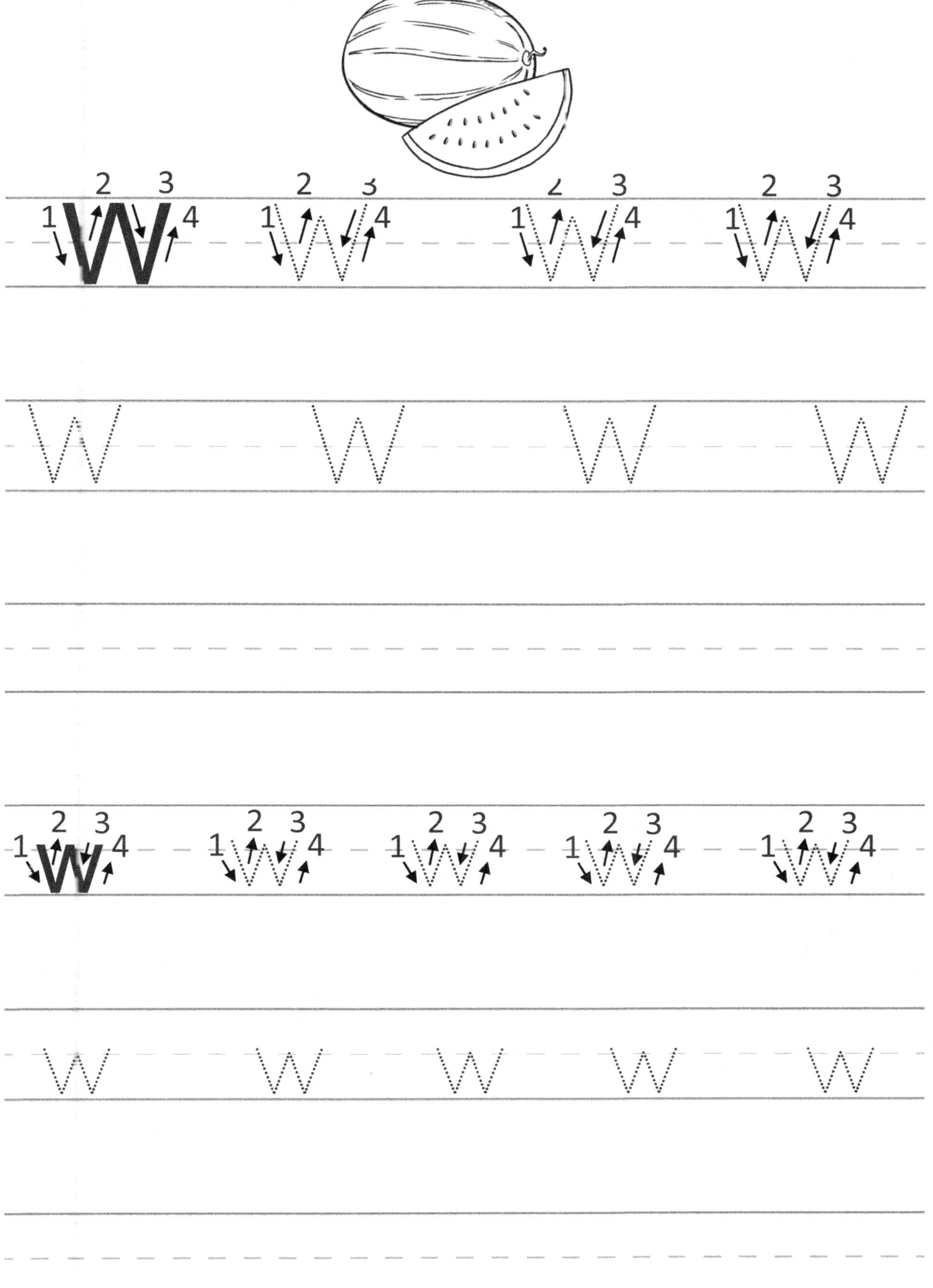

W.E.B. DuBois

Author, Speaker, Freedom Fighter

W.C. Handy

"Father of the Blues", Composer

Wings

Whitney Houston

One of the Bestselling Singers of All-time

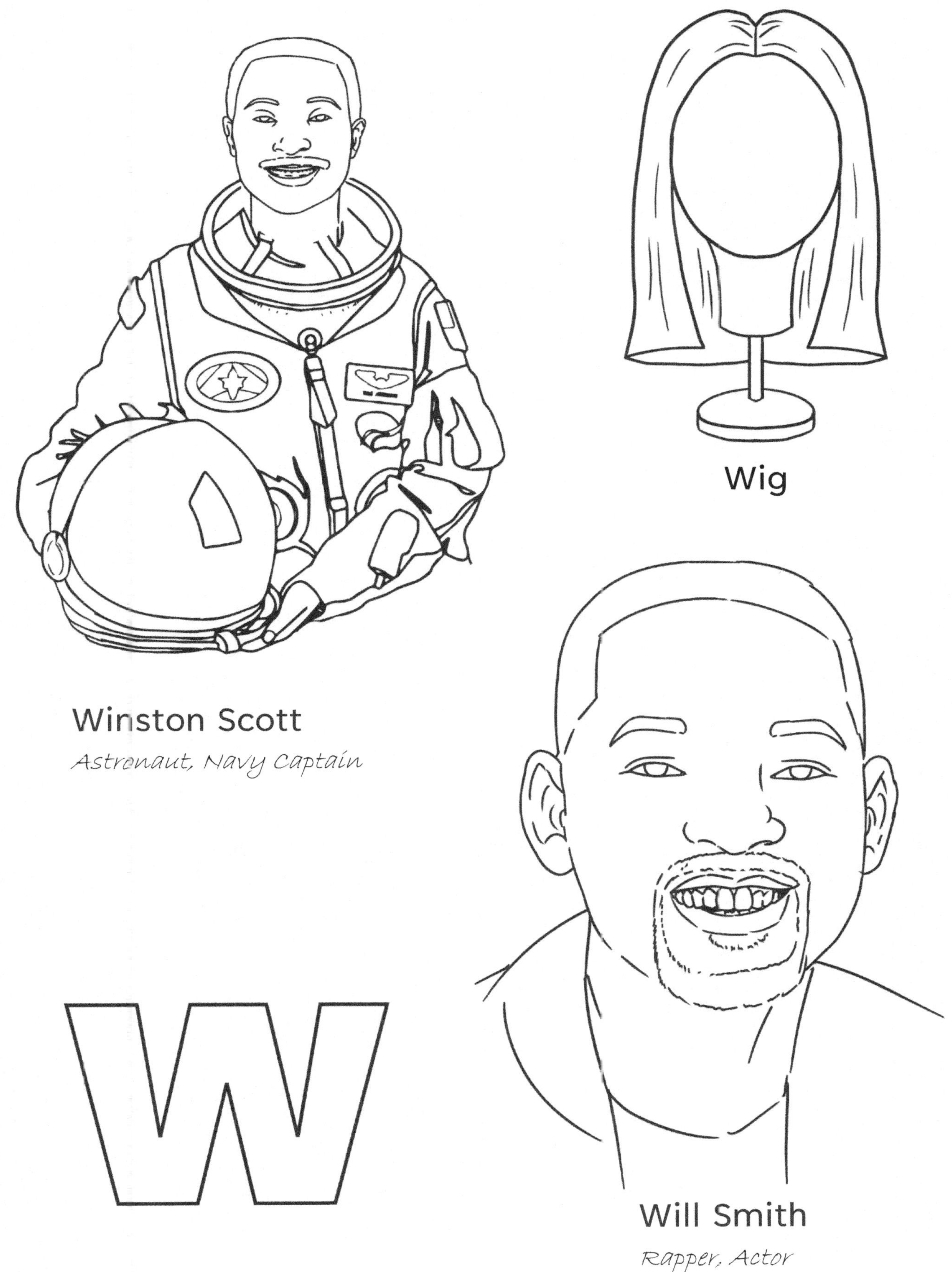

Wig

Winston Scott

Astronaut, Navy Captain

W

Will Smith

Rapper, Actor

1 X 2   1 X 2   1 X 2   1 X 2   1 X 2

X X X X X

1 x 2   1 x 2   1 x 2   1 x 2   1 x 2

x x x x x

1 X 2 1 X 2 1 X 2 1 X 2 1 X 2

X X X X X

1 x 2 1 x 2 1 x 2 1 x 2 1 x 2

x x x x x

Xscape
R&B Group
Xzibit
Rapper, TV Show Host, Radio Host
X-ray
X

XAVIER UNIVERSITY
OF LOUISIANA
Xavier University
HBCU, New Orleans, Louisiana
Xylophone
X
Malcolm X
Minister, Human Rights Activist

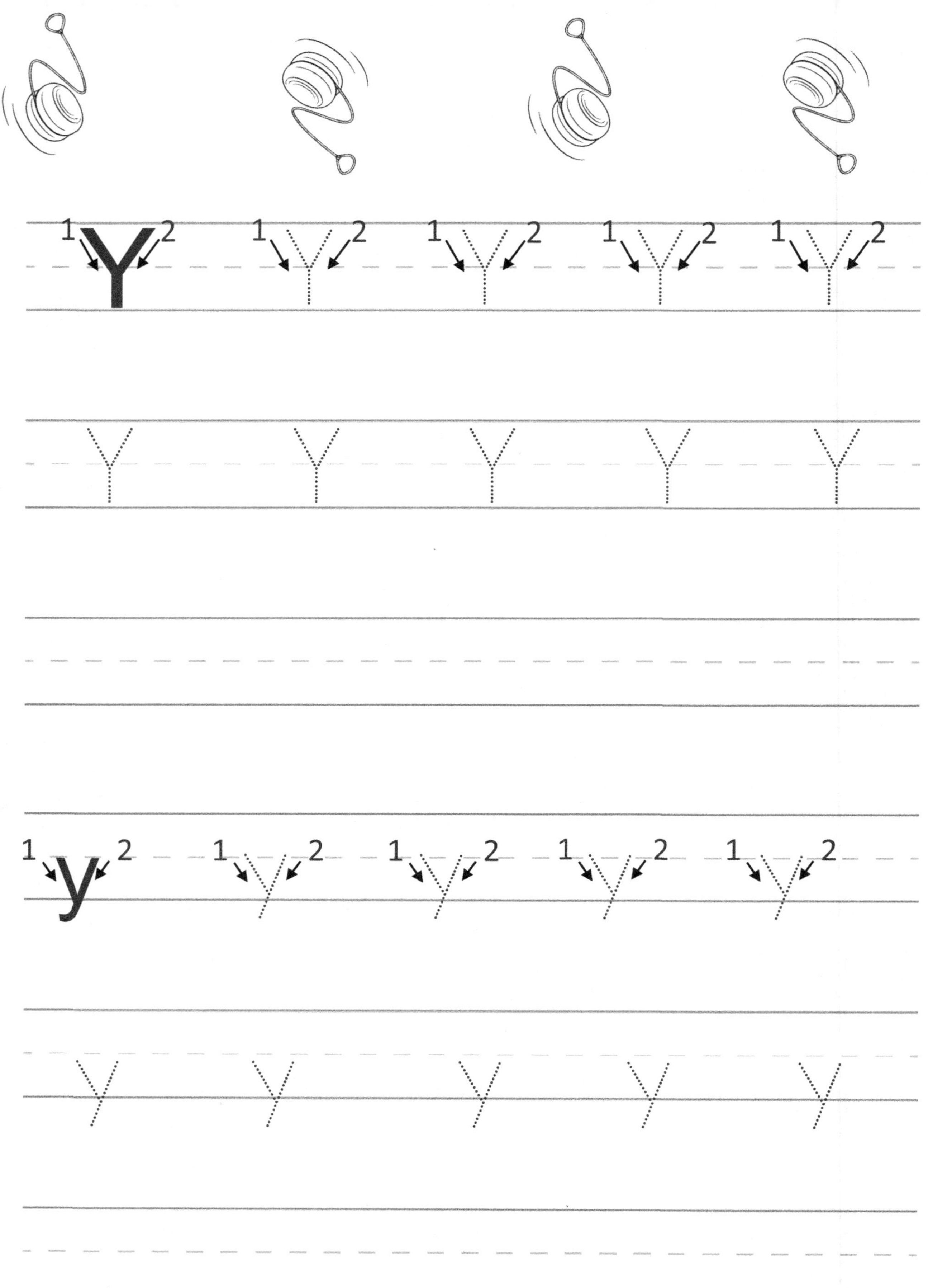
1 Y 2
1 Y 2
1 Y 2
1 Y 2
1 Y 2
Y Y Y Y Y
1 y 2
1 y 2
1 y 2
1 y 2
1 y 2
y y y y y

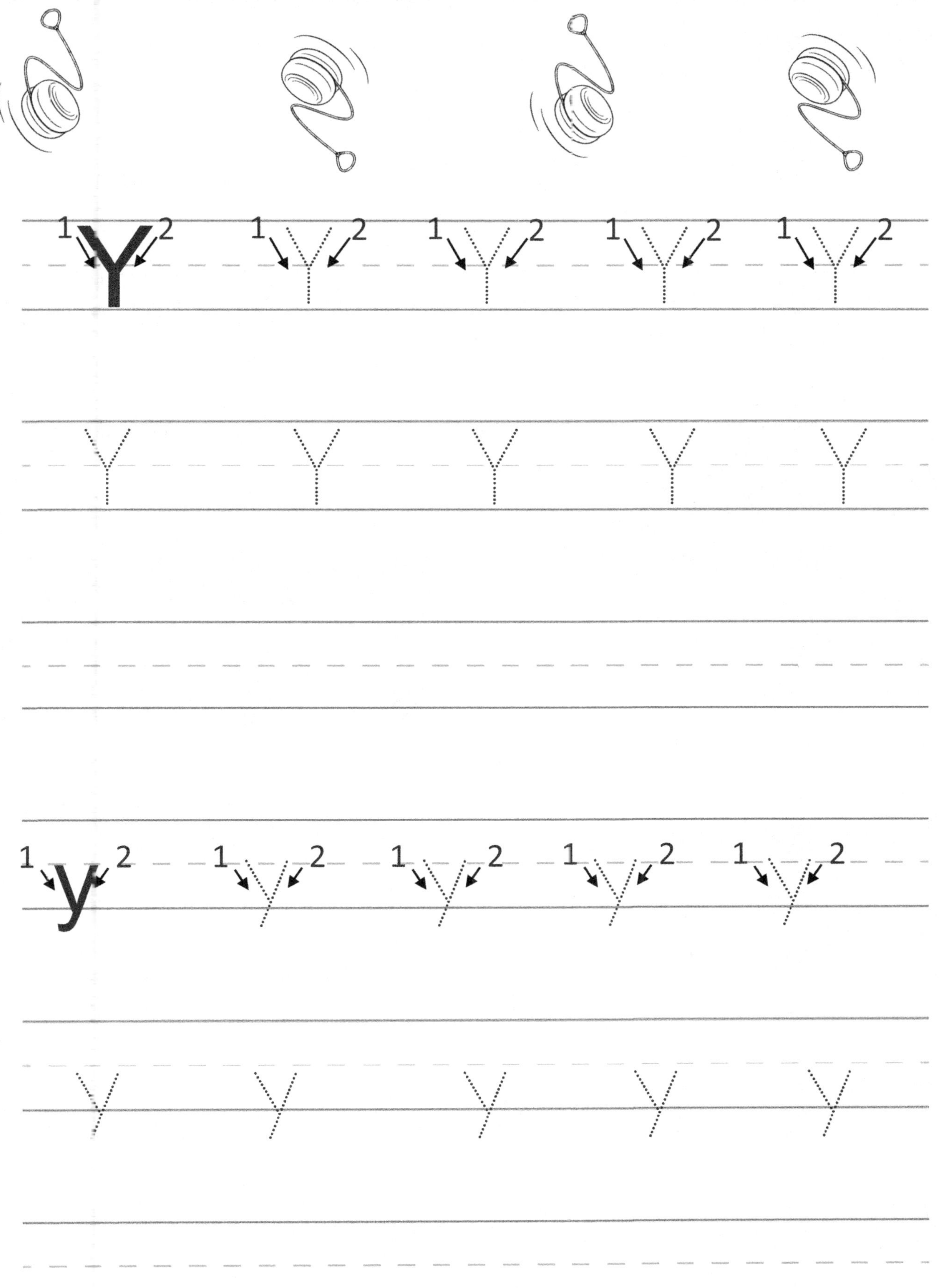

1 Y 2
1 Y 2
1 Y 2
1 Y 2
1 Y 2
Y Y Y Y Y
1 y 2
1 y 2
1 y 2
1 y 2
1 y 2
y y y y y

Yoga

Andrew Young

Former Mayor of Atlanta, Diplomat, Activist

YaYa Girlz

Yaya DaCosta

Actress, Model

YOOOOO!
Yara Shahidi
Actress
Yo
Yams
Y
Yo-Yo
Rapper, Actress

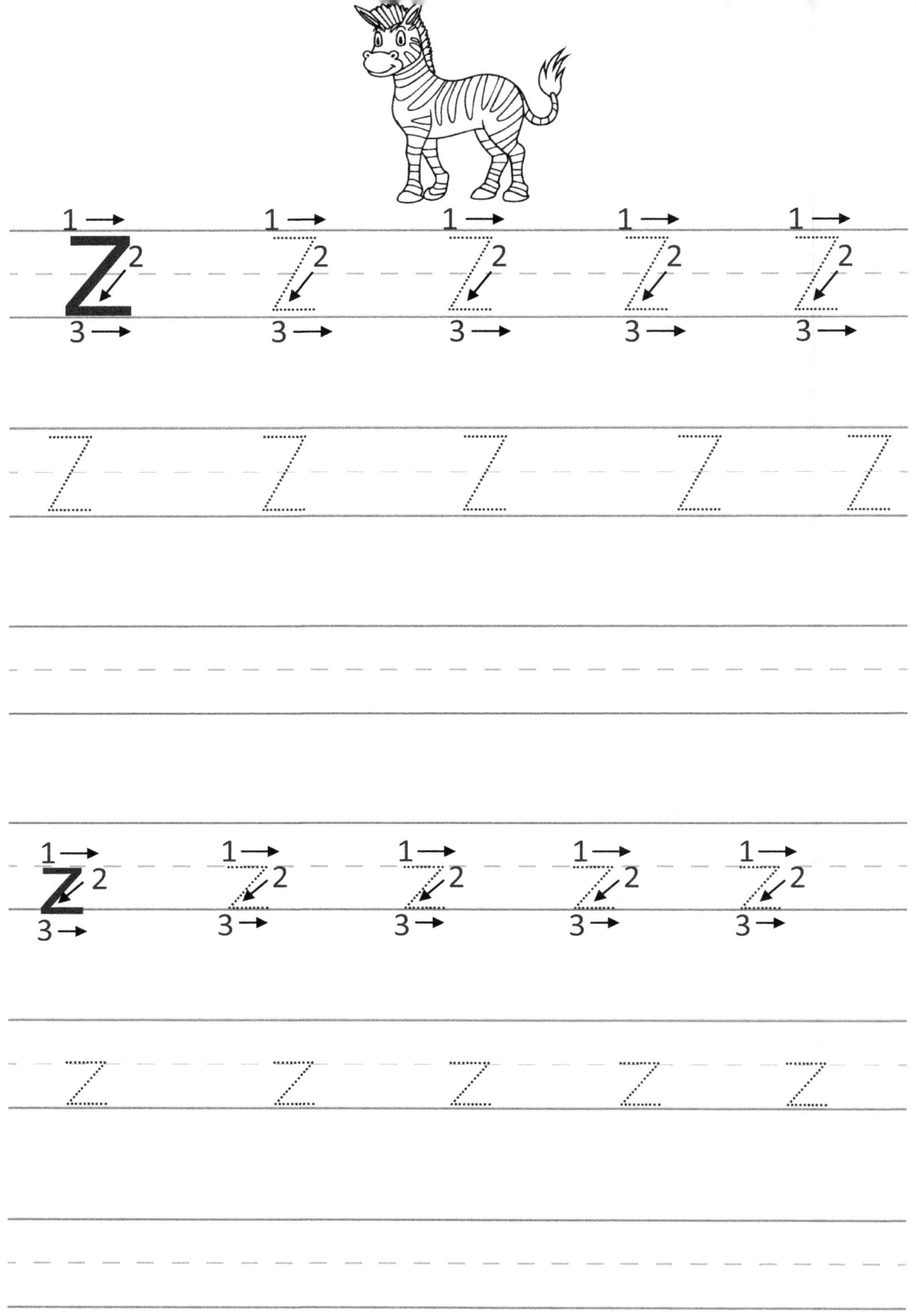
1→
Z 2
3→
1→
2
3→
1→
2
3→
1→
2
3→
1→
2
3→
1→
z 2
3→
1→
2
3→
1→
2
3→
1→
2
3→
1→
2
3→

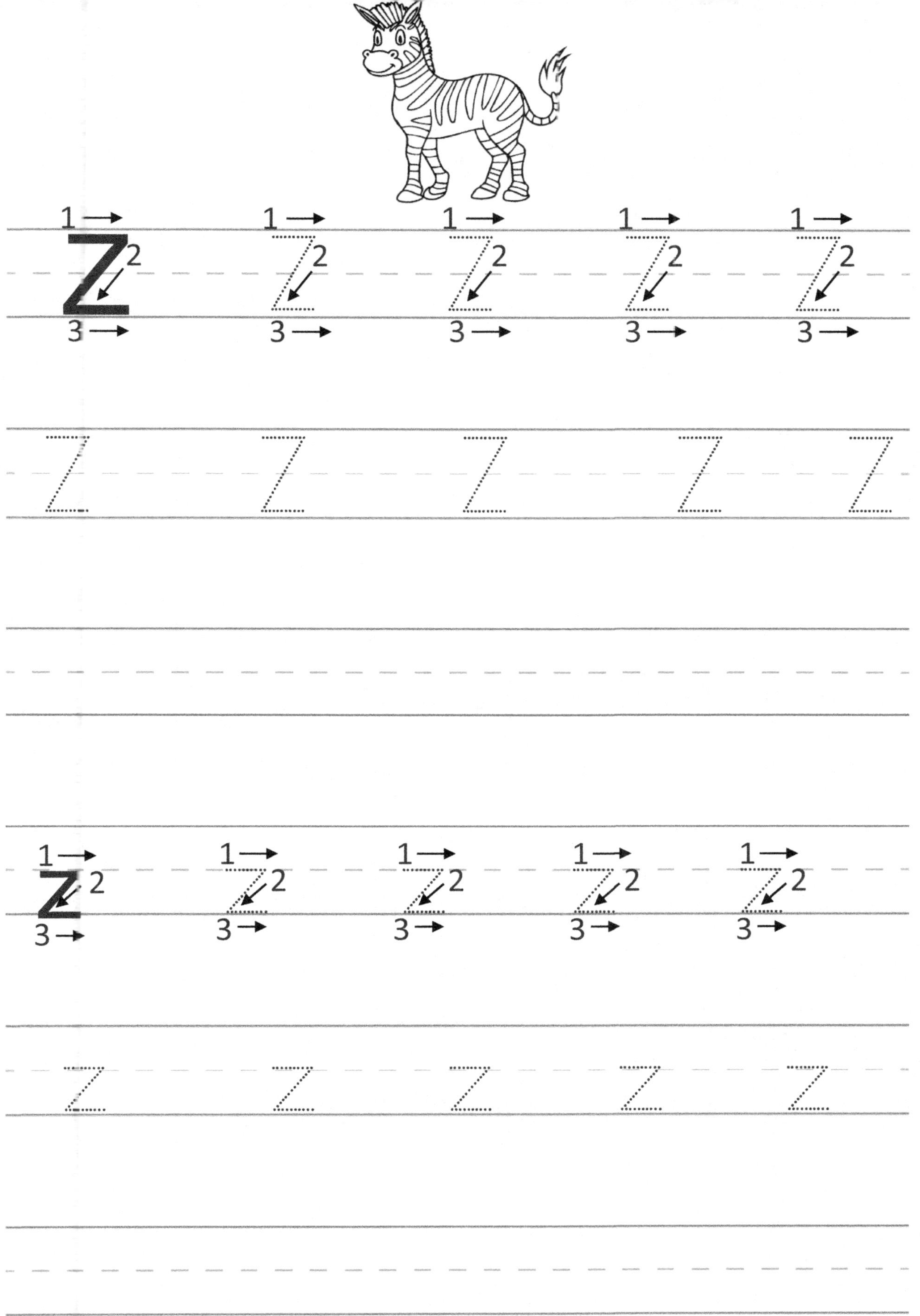

Zaytoven

Record Producer

Zora Neale Hurston

Author, Filmmaker

Empress Zewditu

Only Empress of the Ethiopian Empire

Zydeco

Music that Blends Blues and R&B

Zoë Kravitz

Actress and Model

Zeta Phi Beta

A Divine Nine Sorority

Zulu Warrior

Brave Fighters of Zulu Kingdom

The ankh is an

Ancient Egyptian

symbol.

The ankh symbolizes life. It is sometimes called the key of life.

Trace the picture of an ankh from ancient Egypt.

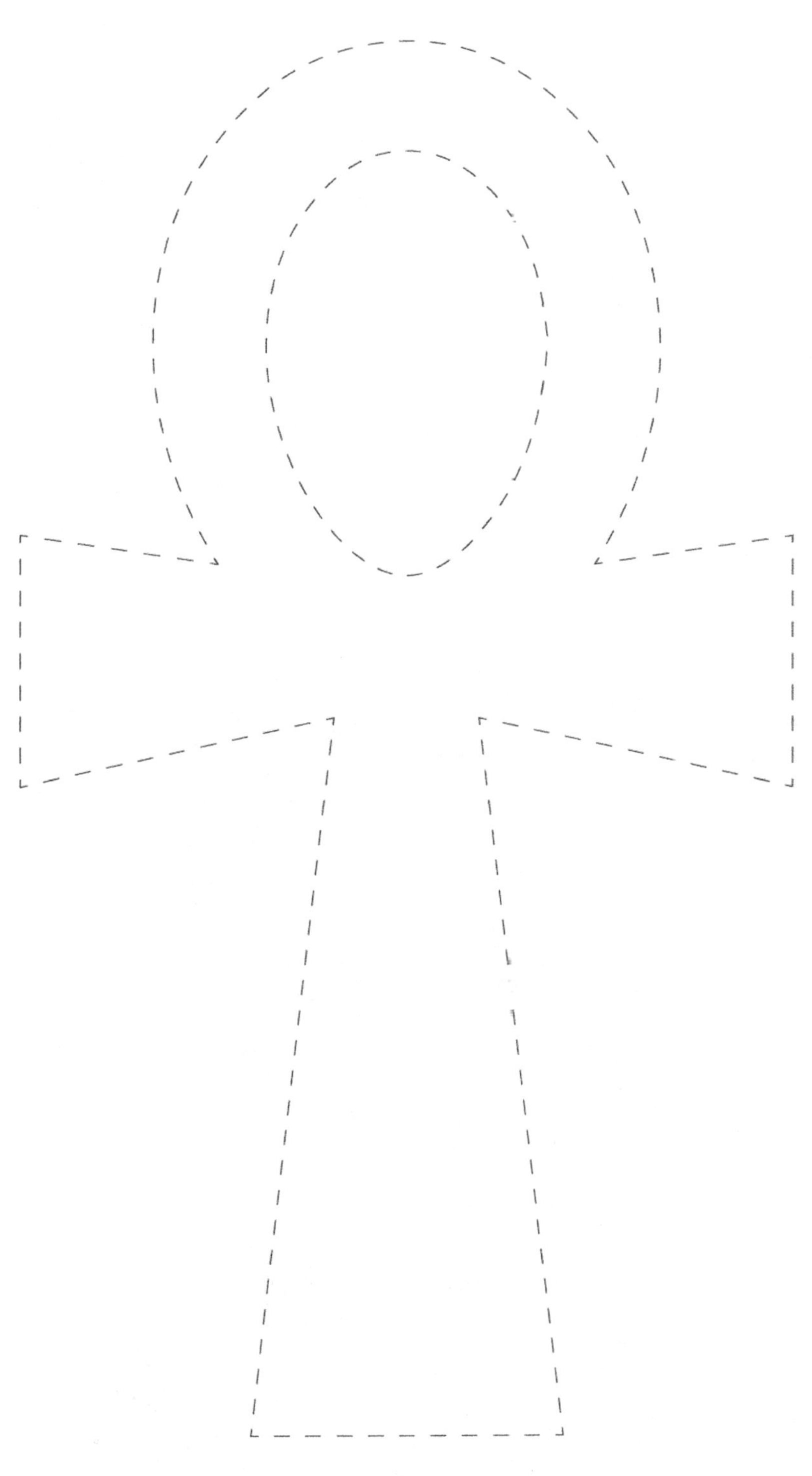

Afro puffs are a

natural hairstyle.

Draw a picture of a boy with an afro or a girl with afro puffs.

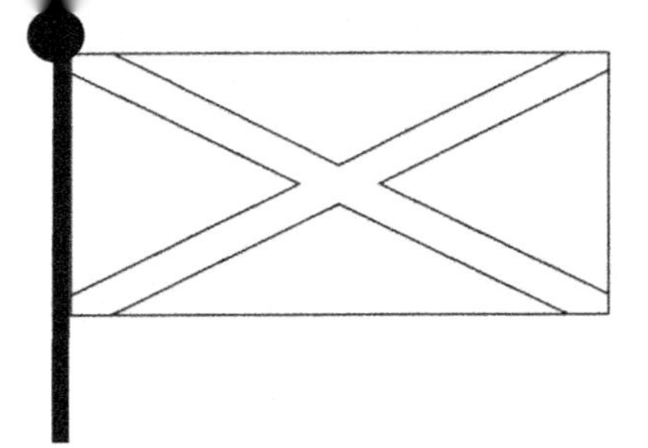

Bob Marley was a

Jamaican born

singer/songwriter.

Bob Marley was a young Jamaican who wrote and sang very popular Reggae songs. In the song 'One Love' he sings about love and unity for all people. He recorded 15 albums by age 36.

Color 'One Love' using red, yellow, and green.

Breakdancing

or breaking is a

type of dance.

Breakdancing is a high energy type of dance. Black and Latinx people use head spins, back spins, and fancy footwork. It started in the 1960s in New York City.

Color the dancer in front of the brick wall.

Charles Drew was

a surgeon and

medical researcher.

While studying to be the first black doctor to graduate from Columbia University in 1940, Dr. Charles Drew found new ways to save blood. During World War II, this was very important because injured soldiers were so far away from hospitals.

There are 5 capital B's below. Circle them using red.

Coconut oil from

the coconut fruit

has many uses.

Coconut oil is a natural moisturizer we use to keep our curls poppin' and skin moisturized.

Color the hairstyles.

The djembe is a

drum from West

Africa.

The djembe (said *gem-bay*) is a drum from West Africa that symbolizes people coming together in peace. It is played with bare hands.

Look at the picture of the djembe on *page 15**, then draw the instrument you see.*

A drumline is the

heart and soul of

a marching band.

Drumlines are called the heartbeat of marching bands. They only use instruments that strike one part of the instrument against another to create sound. Drumlines use bass drums, snare drums, quads, and cymbals.

Color the drumline below.

Eatonville is a

city in the state

of Florida.

Eatonville is a city about 20 minutes from Disney World in Florida. It was the first all-Black town in the United States, created by newly freed slaves in 1887.

Use pretty spring colors (pink, yellow, purple, and blue) to bring the flowers to life.

The Edmund Pettus

Bridge is in

Selma, Alabama.

The Edmund Pettus Bridge is where Freedom Fighters crossed going from Selma to Montgomery in support of voting rights for Black people in 1965. Activists Dr. Martin Luther King, Jr. and John Lewis led the march.

Write the name of the bridge between the arrows.

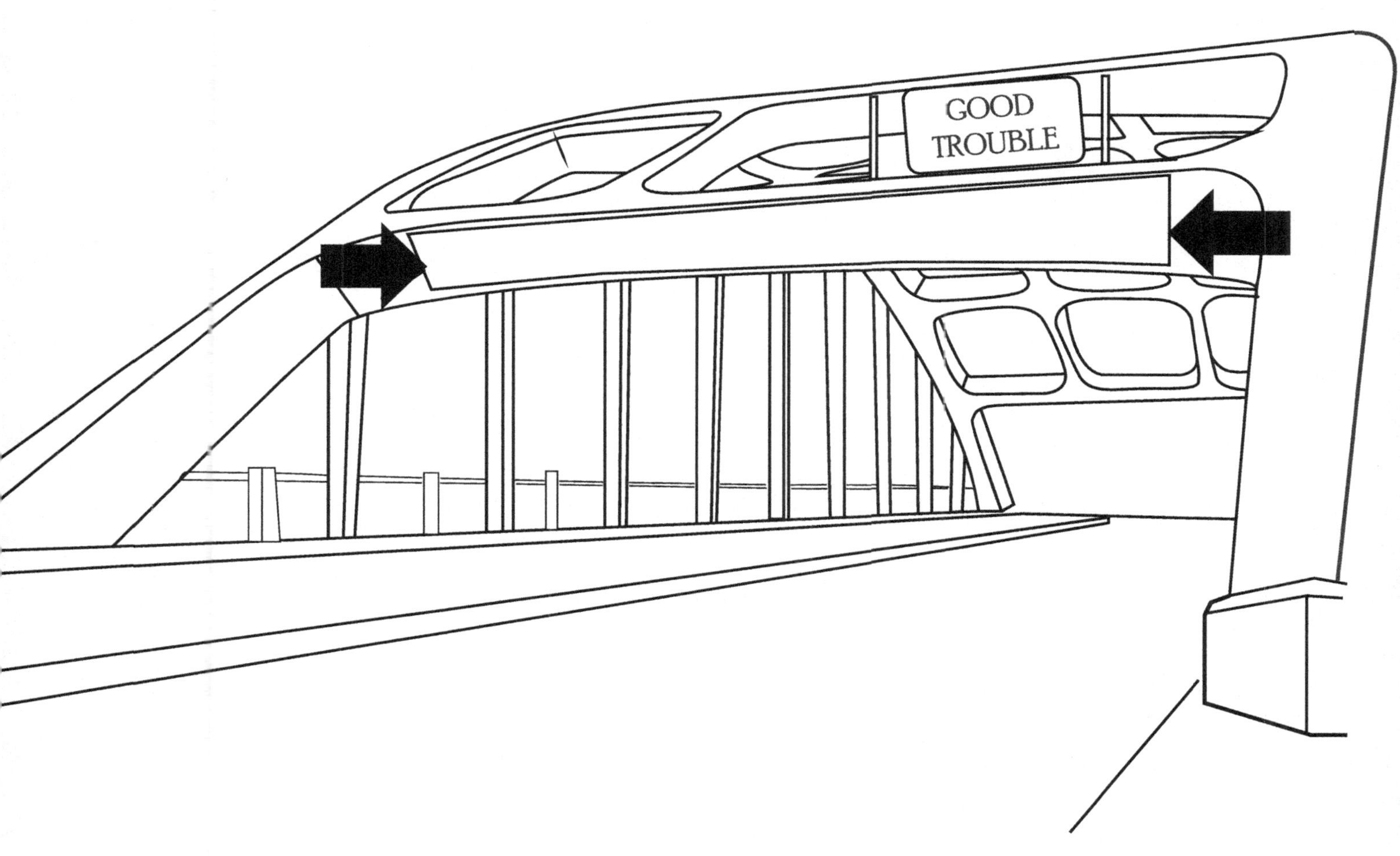

Hey, hey, hey! It's

the Fat Albert

cartoon.

‘Fat Albert’ was a very popular Black cartoon in the 1970s. In each show, he and his friends learned an important life lesson.

Search ‘Fat Albert’ and draw a picture of one character.

FAMU is a university

with a rattler

as its mascot.

Florida A&M University, also called FAMU, is an HBCU (Historically Black College or University) in Tallahassee, Florida. It is said that FAMU sits on the highest of seven hills.

Find the highest hill and write FAMU in orange and green.

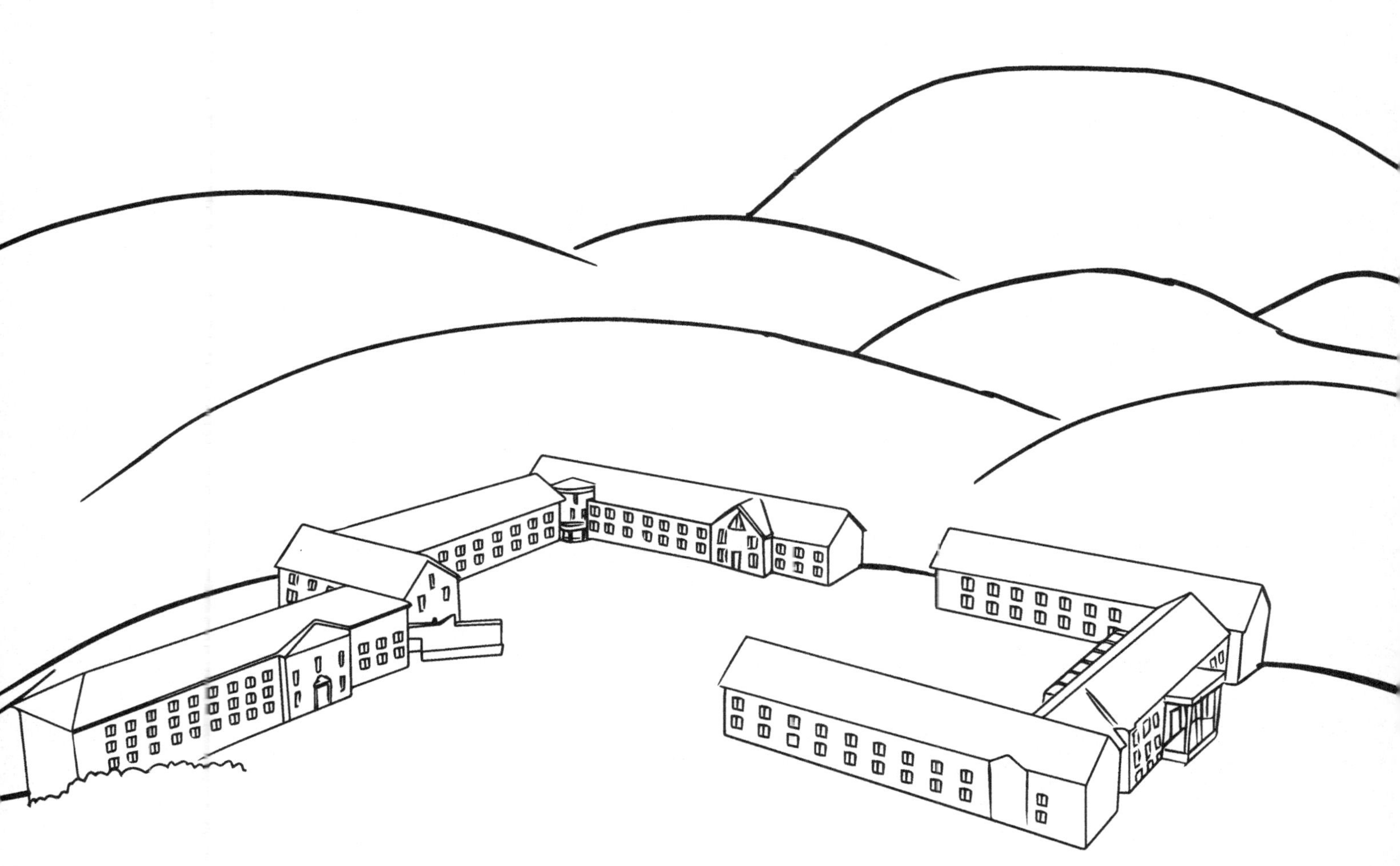

George W. Carver

was a scientist

from Missouri.

George Washington Carver was a professor at Tuskegee University for 47 years. He discovered over 300 uses for peanuts, some you see here.

Color the items you know.

Greenwood District in Tulsa, Oklahoma was one of the wealthiest Black communities in the United States in the early 1900s. O.W. Gurley started Greenwood, also called 'Black Wall Street,' when he bought 40 acres of land to encourage Black excellence. All of the businesses were Black-owned.

Color the different businesses O.W. Gurley visited spending a day in Greenwood District.

O.W. Gurley, founder of Greenwood District.

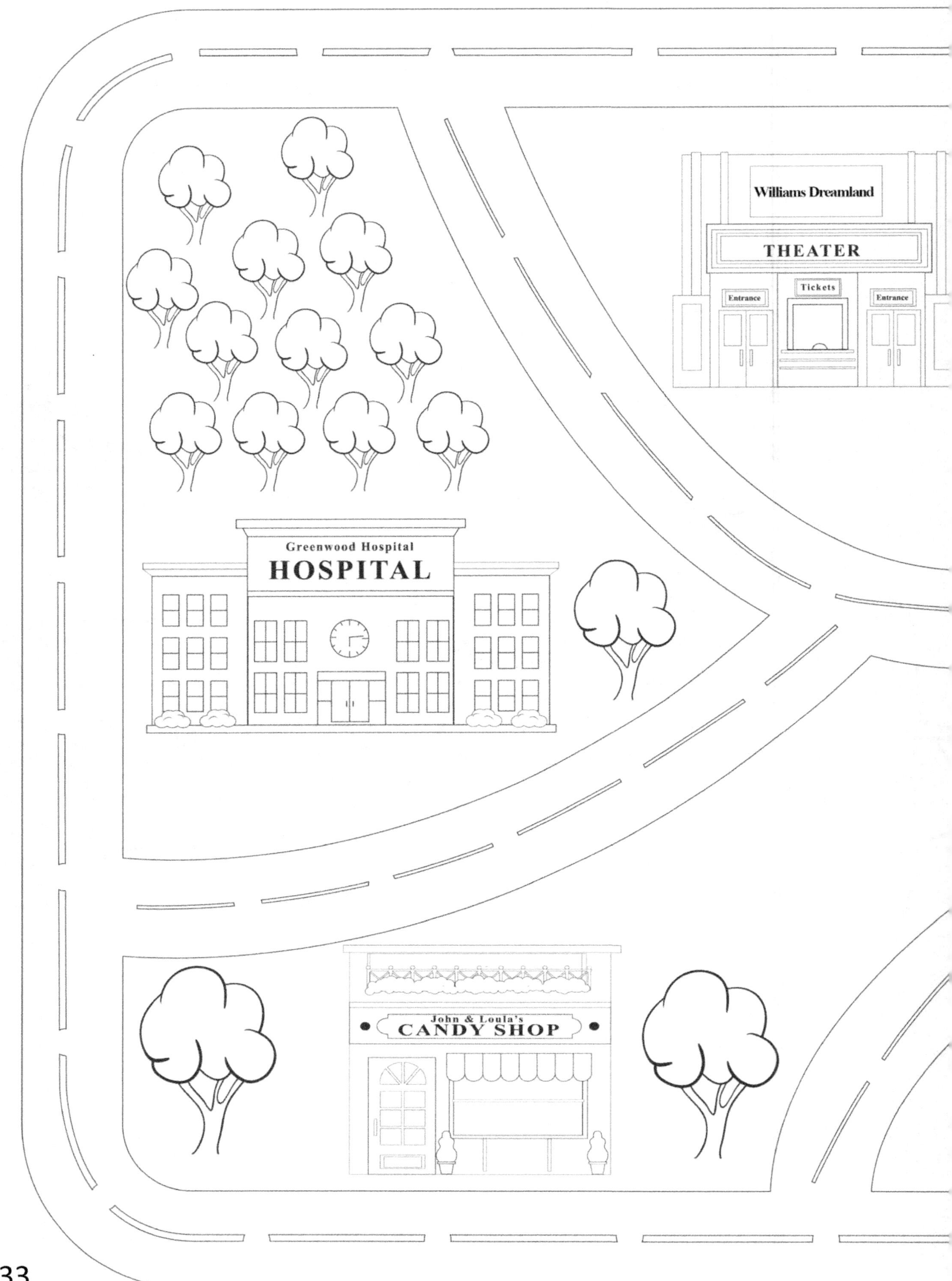
Williams Dreamland
THEATER
Tickets
Entrance
Entrance
Greenwood Hospital
HOSPITAL
John & Loula's
CANDY SHOP

Booker T. Washington
High School
Berry's Taxi Service
TAXI

The Harlem

Renaissance was

a very fun time.

The Harlem Renaissance was a time of understanding Black culture through books, art, music, dance, fashion, and theater. It took place in the 1920s and 1930s in Harlem, New York.

Circle the activities you like to do.

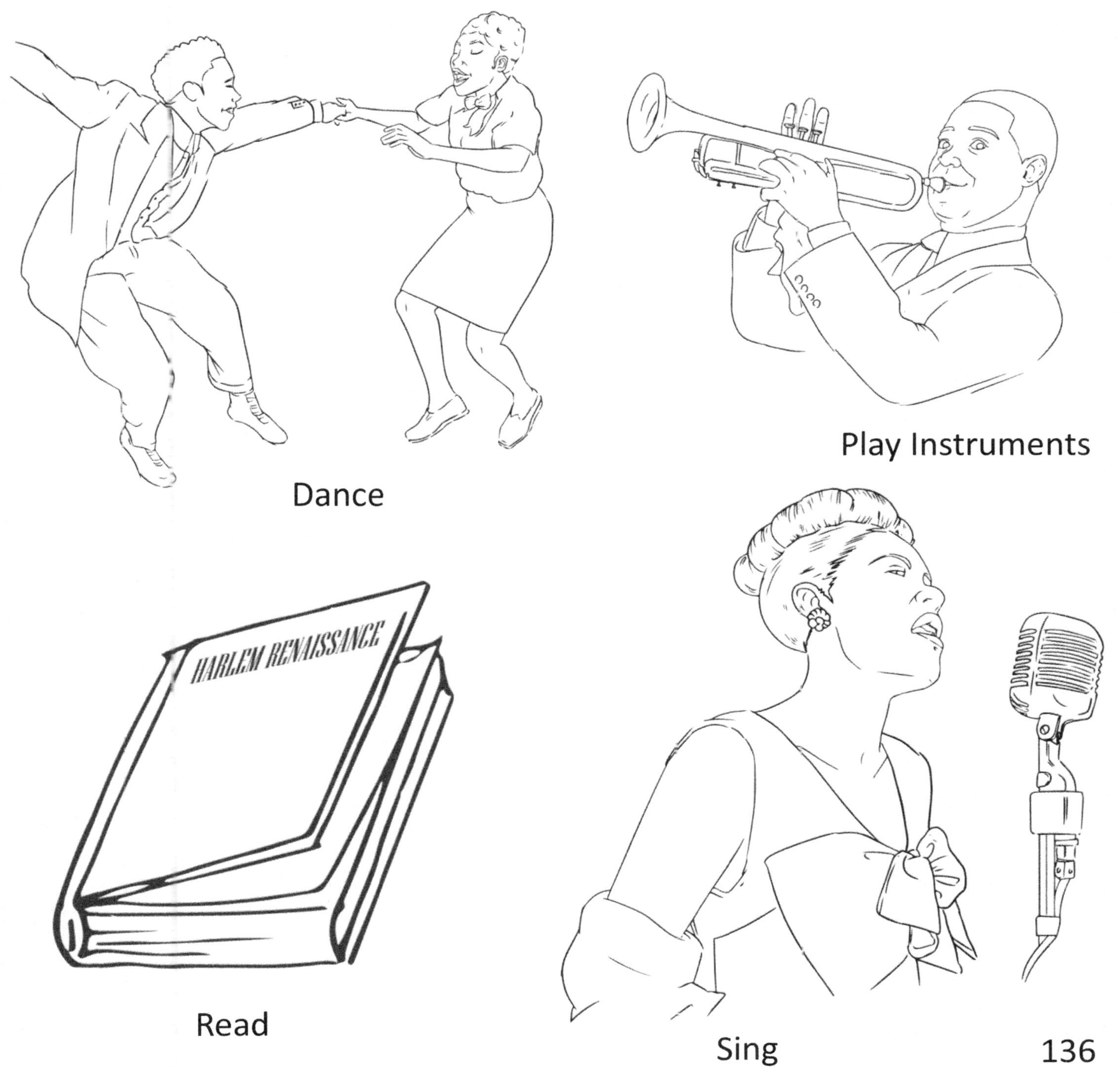

Dance

Play Instruments

Read

Sing

Hercules Posey

was the first Black

President's chef.

Chef to Pres. George Washington, Hercules Posey was widely admired for his cooking skills. He brought foods to Washington, D.C. from all over the country such as salted New England cod fish, prized Connecticut onions, New York cheese, and Carolina rice.

Draw lines from the pictures to their names.

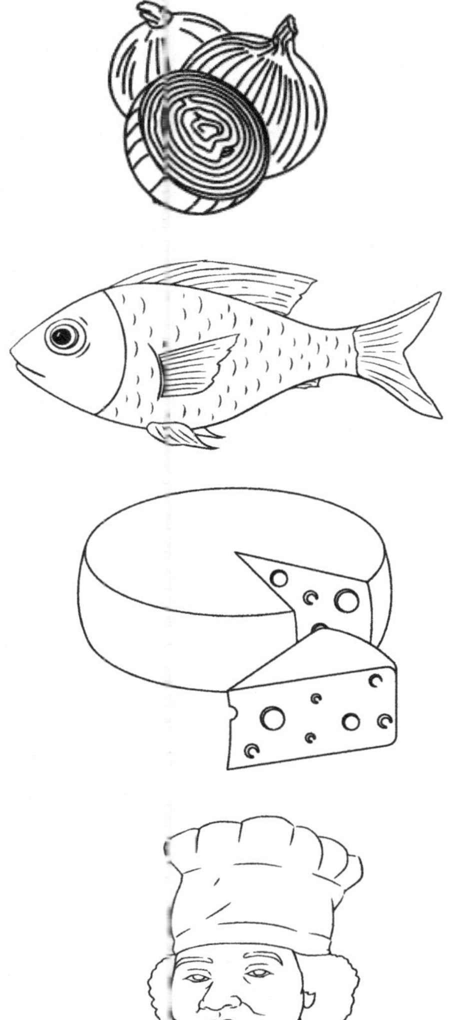

cheese

onions

Hercules Posey

fish

"I have a dream today," said Dr. Martin Luther King.

The “I Have A Dream” speech was given in Washington, D.C. by Dr. King in 1963. He hoped to inspire an end to racism so everyone and every race could get along.

Color the way you imagine he looked on that day.

The ironing board

was improved by

a Black woman.

Sarah Boone was a Black dress maker who wanted a better way to iron dresses for her clients. On April 26, 1892, she was awarded a patent for the ironing board as the first Black woman to receive a patent.

Unscramble the letters to name each picture.

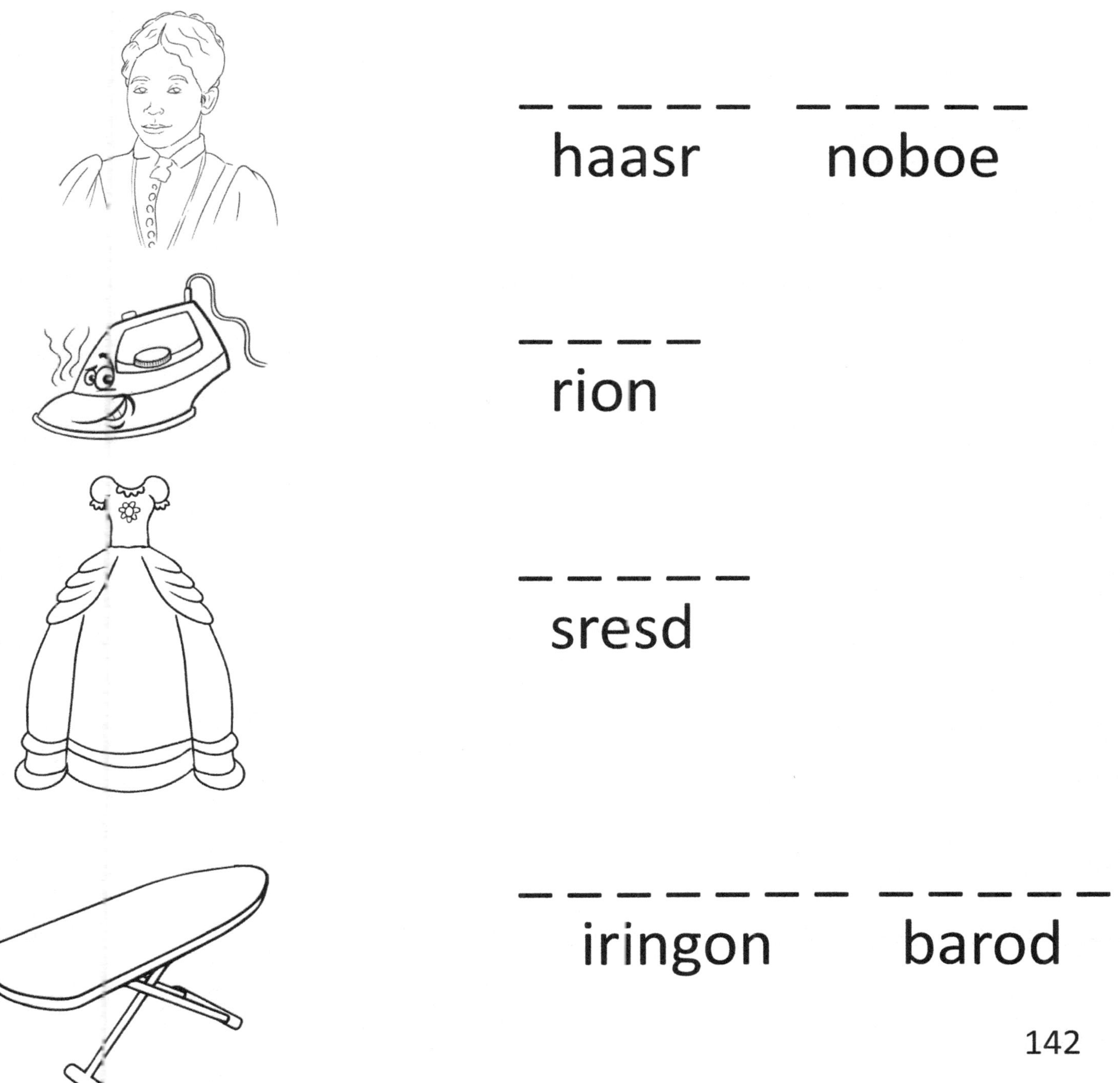

Jackie Robinson

wore the number

42 on his jersey.

Jackie Robinson was the first Black man to play professional baseball. He played for the Brooklyn Dodgers for 10 seasons and wore the number 42 on his jersey.

Trace the home run path Jackie Robinson ran while playing.

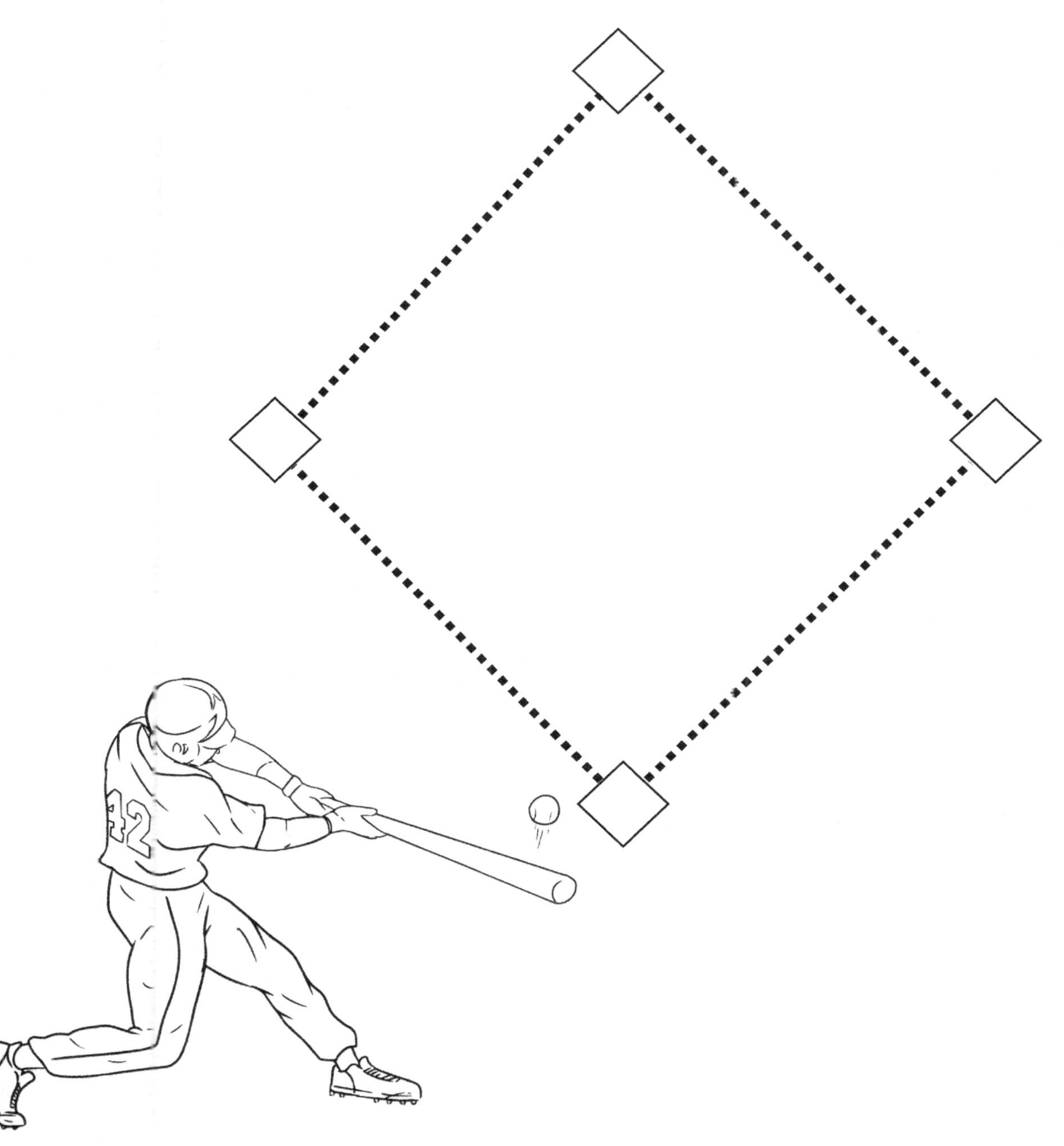

Jazz is music

that uses many

instruments.

Jazz is a type of music that originated in the Black hang out spots where people liked to dance. It uses many instruments.

Color the instruments below.

Kwanzaa is a

celebration of

Black culture.

Kwanzaa is a celebration of family, culture, and community helping African-Americans reconnect with their African roots. It covers seven principles one each day from December 26th to January 1st.

Color the three candles on the left red, the three candles on the right green, and the center candle black.

Kente cloth is

a type of hand

woven fabric.

The colorful patterned strips of cotton and silk being placed over and under each other trace back to the Asante people in what is now Ghana.

Color each pattern using bright colors. Then repeat the color patterns on identical layouts.

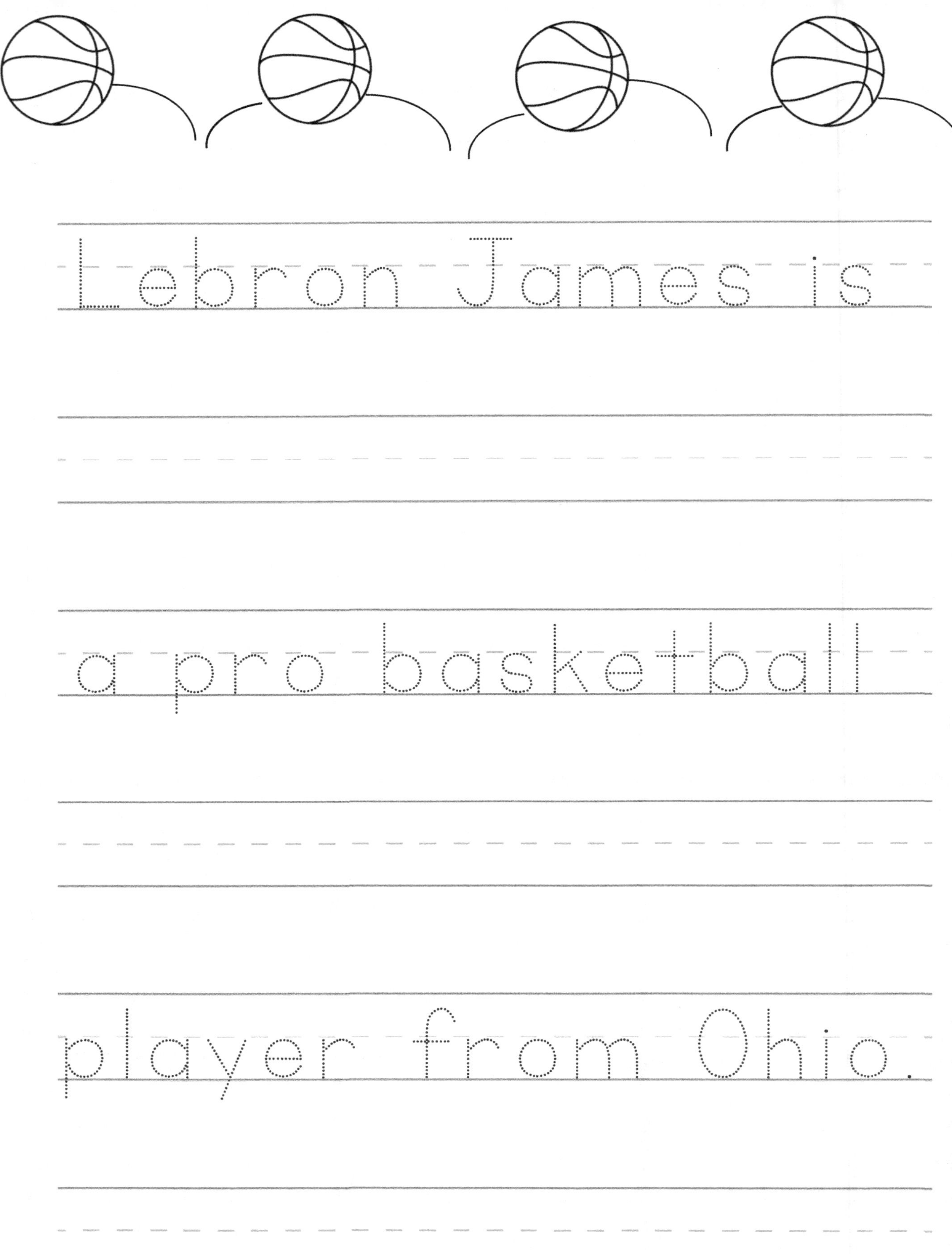

Lebron James is

a pro basketball

player from Ohio.

Lebron James led the Cleveland Cavaliers to their first NBA Championship in 2016.

Color his celebration.

Lion families are

from Africa,

called prides.

Leo the lion got lost from his pride. Help Leo find his family roaming on the continent of Africa.

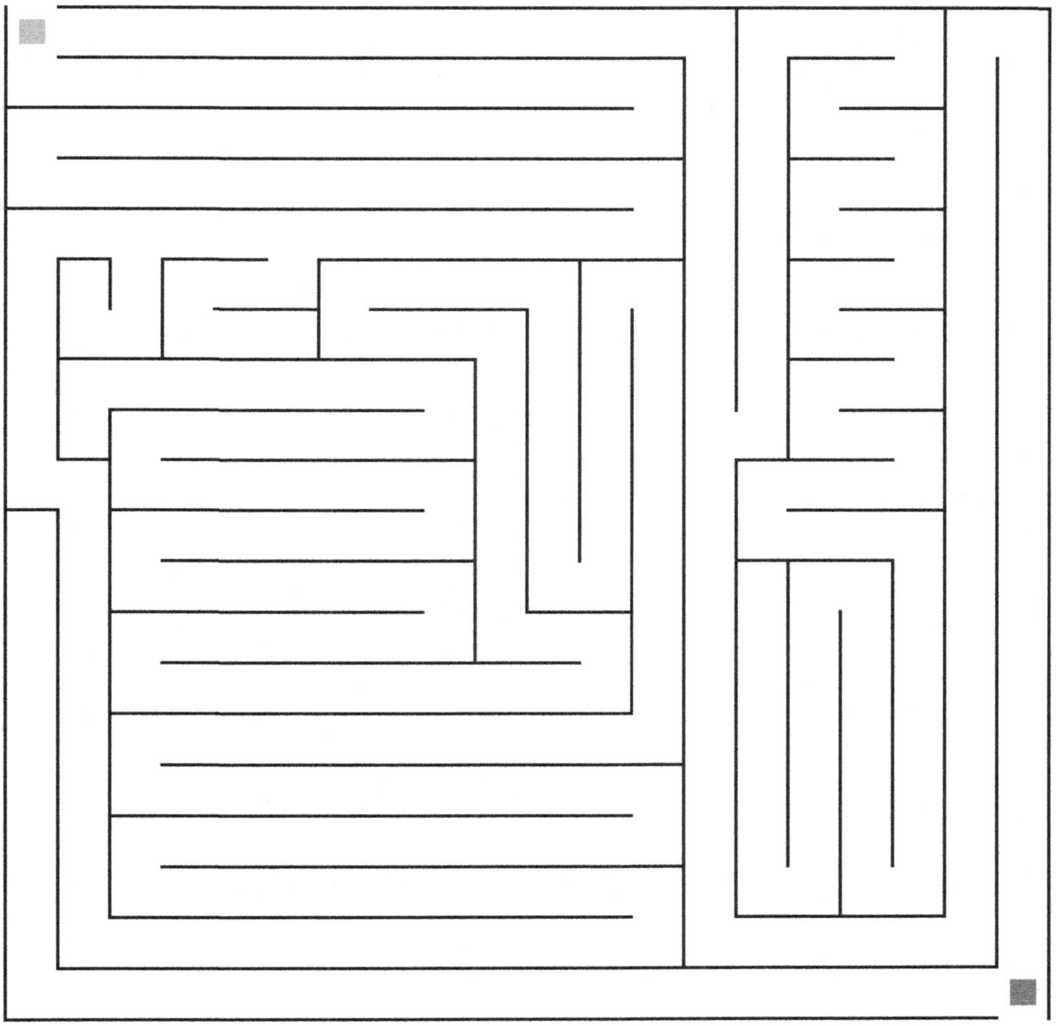

The first Black

woman in space

was Mae Jemison.

Mae Jemison is an astronaut who went around Earth 8 times.

Count the stars floating around her.

Mary McLeod

Bethune has a

statue in D.C.

Mary McLeod Bethune was the founder of Daytona Literary and Industrial Training School for Negro Girls, an all-girls school that stands today as Bethune-Cookman University. To raise money to start the school in 1904, she sold sweet potato pies, ice cream, and fried fish.

Draw pictures of each.

Nefertiti was a

queen in Ancient

Egypt.

Queen Nefertiti was from Nubia, an area in Egypt in 1370 BC. She helped her husband, Pharaoh Akhenaten, make important decisions. She was known as one of the most beautiful women to have ever lived.

Search a picture of Queen Nefertiti and sketch her image.

The Nile River

is the longest

river in the world.

The Nile River is 4,160 miles long and stretches through 11 countries in Africa such as Kenya and Rwanda. Local citizens live only a few miles from the river because the area is desert which is completely dry. However, land near the Nile is green and allows crops to grow, animals to eat, and people to fish.

Color this picture of Ancient Egypt.

Oprah Winfrey

started her own

cable TV channel.

Oprah is a TV and film producer, author, talk show host, and gift giver who sprinkles her Black Girl Magic all around. Her favorite color is green.

There are 4 capital O's below. Circle them using green.

Leontyne Price is

an opera singer

born in 1927.

Known as America's greatest soprano, Leontyne Price began playing piano at 3 and singing at 8. She sang opera all over the world and was praised internationally. She was awarded the Presidential Medal of Freedom in 1964.

Color her image.

Pharell Williams

is a well-known

music producer.

Pharell is best known for making music and beats. He got his shot after performing in a high school talent show. He helps other rappers and singers by writing lyrics for them to sing and rap, along with creating the music.

Color the 1…purple, color the 2…blue, and the 3…pink.

Most pyramids

were built in

ancient Egypt.

Egyptian pyramids were built as tombs, or burial places, for pharaohs, their wives, and companions. They are four equal triangles put together. The Pyramid of Khufu was built to stand 481 feet in the air and took 27 years to finish. It sits next to two other, smaller pyramids near the Nile river.

Trace a path around the pyramids below.

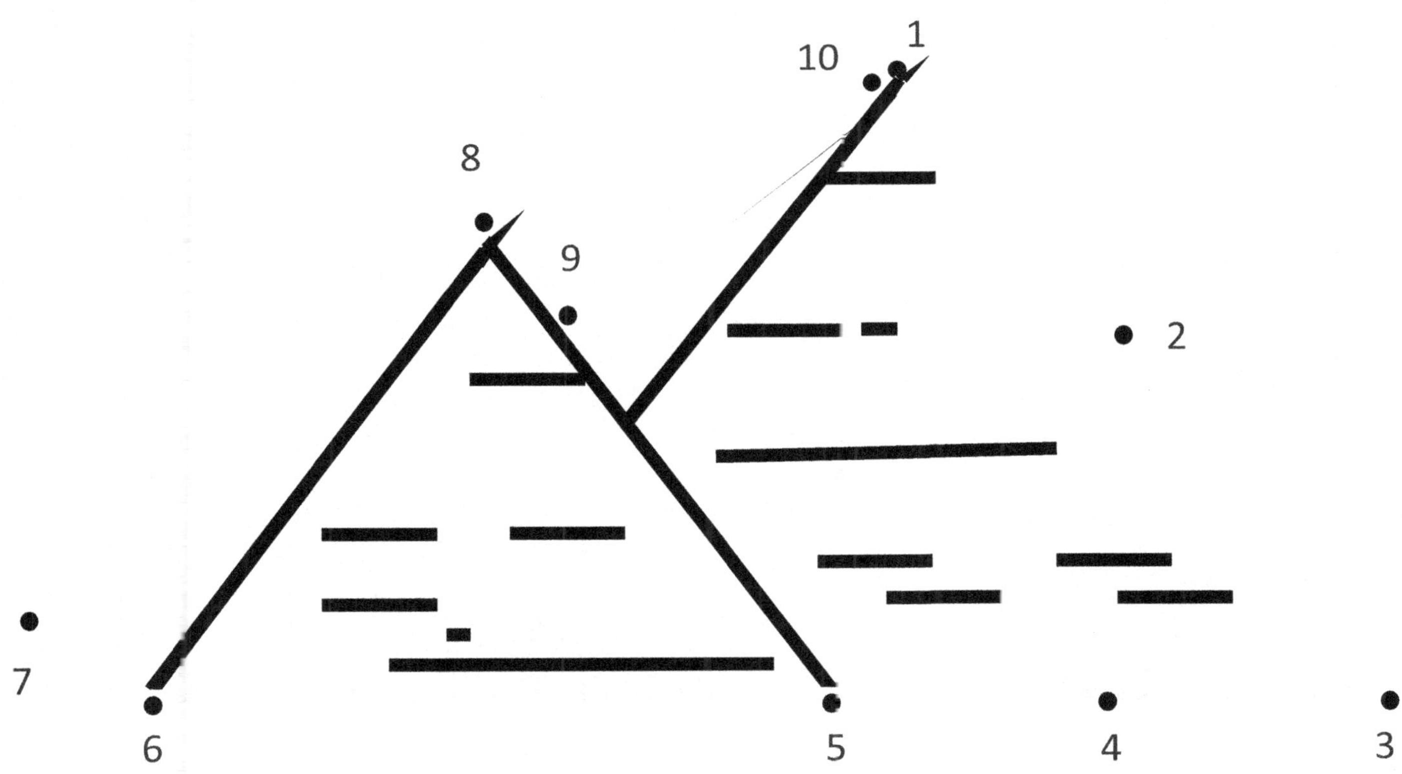

Queen Latifah

released her first

album in Nov. 1989.

Queen Latifah is a well-known actress and rapper. Rap is like telling a story or saying a poem to music.

Make up a poem, then perform it.

Que-dog is a

nickname for

Omega men.

Omega Psi Phi Fraternity is a group of esteemed men, like brothers. The organization was started in 1911 at Howard University. Nicknamed Que-dogs, this brotherhood represents manhood, education, not giving up, and uplifting each other.

Color his clothes in purple and gold (or yellow), signature Omega colors.

Reggae music

originated in the

1960s in Jamaica.

Reggae has a very distinct sound. It uses many instruments, mainly the guitar, keyboard, trumpet, and drums. Reggae is usually about love, religion, and day-to-day life. Bob Marley was a famous Reggae singer.

Color the 1…red, color the 2…yellow, and the 3…green.

Ruby Bridges

began school

all by herself.

Ruby Bridges was 6 years old when she went to kindergarten. In the southern states, Black and White students went to different schools. Ruby Bridges was the first Black to attend school with White children in her area. She was very brave.

Color Ruby and her parents as they get her ready for school.

Sankofa means

go back and get

it, learn a lesson.

Sankofa is from a collection of Adinkra symbols with meanings from Ghana. The symbols are stamped on fabric worn by leaders during important times such as weddings, festivals, and naming ceremonies. Sankofa has two symbols which both mean learn lessons from your mistakes.

Draw a box around the Sankofa you like best.

Jan Matzeliger

knew how to

make shoes.

Growing up, Jan Matzeliger learned how to make containers, ornaments, and metal tools while hanging out at his dad's shop. He learned how to make shoes by hand. Only wealthy people owned them because shoes cost a lot of money to make. In 1882, he invented a machine that could make 700 pairs of shoes a day! So, everyone could afford shoes. He changed the shoe industry forever.

Color Jan Matzeliger next to his shoe-lasting machine.

The Nicholas

Brothers were a

tap dancing duo.

Fayard taught himself and his brother, Nicholas, how to dance watching other entertainers. The Nicholas Brothers performed their tap dancing and acrobatic jumping moves in movies, TV shows, and on stages everywhere.

Color The Nicholas Brothers doing a stunt dance move below.

The traffic

light used to only

have two colors.

Before Garrett A. Morgan's invention in 1923, traffic lights only had two signals, stop (red) and go (green). Morgan added a third signal, a blinking yellow light to warn drivers to slow down before stopping. This helped to prevent so many car accidents.

Color the traffic light for Mr. Morgan, then color the matching meaning.

Underground

Railroad trails

went to Canada.

Harriet Tubman was a brave woman who made many trips from the South to the North taking slaves to freedom on the Underground Railroad. It was not a train, but several trails with stops at friendly houses along the way. Slaves used lamps and the North Star to know where to go.

Circle the arrows that point up toward the north part of the map.

Usain Bolt holds

three Olympic

track records.

Usain Bolt is one of the fastest people to ever live! By age 12, everyone in his town knew he was the fastest sprinter on the island of Jamaica. He has 23 gold medals, 19 on tracks around the world.

Color Usain winning this race.

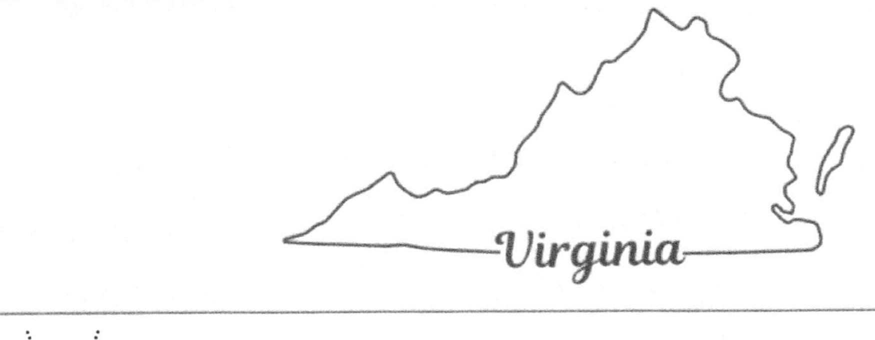

Virginia was a

slave state where

“Box” Brown lived.

Henry "Box" Brown was an enslaved magician who freed himself. With help, he shipped himself in a box from Richmond, Virginia to Philadelphia, Pennsylvania, where Black people were free. The trip took 27 hours and when he arrived, he became a free man.

Trace Henry "Box" Brown's name on the box.

Vanessa Williams

was the first

Black Ms. America.

Vanessa Williams is an actress, singer, and fashion designer. She was introduced to the world in 1984 as the first Black Miss America in the pageant's 63-year history.

Draw a winner's crown on Miss America's head.

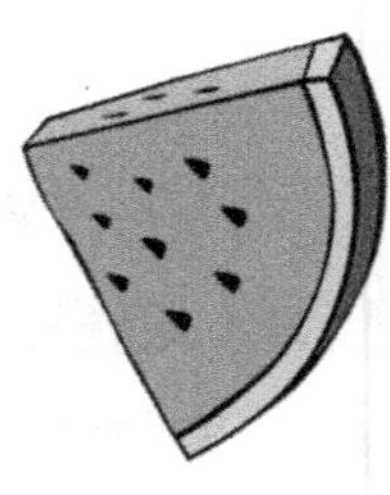

Watermelon is a

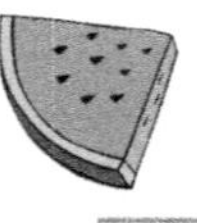

yummy fruit that

is healthy.

Watermelon is a sweet, red fruit grown in the southern states of Florida, Georgia, and Texas. Freed Black men and women grew and sold watermelon to make money for their families. To us, watermelon is a symbol of prosperity and dignity.

Connect the dots to see what the picture reveals.

Wraps are

protective and

stylish for hair.

Wraps serve many purposes. They promote healthier hair, and keep braided and curled styles in place. Wraps also match outfits. Erykah Badu, a singer, is known to wear wraps to match her clothes.

Decorate her wrap using two colors.

Xavier University

is a Black school

in New Orleans.

Xavier University of Louisiana is an HBCU, or Historically Black College or University. It is one of the top Black schools teaching health sciences and math. It was founded in 1925 and its pharmacy school was founded in 1927.

Finish sketching the Xavier University gate and don't forget to write the name.

YaYa Girlz is a

group of girls

who are friends.

YaYa Girlz was created by Carla DuPont because her daughter, author Cameron Alexa, did not have shirts with pictures of Black girls on them. Each one of the girls represents a different complexion and a different style so all Black girls see a character that looks like them.

Go to www.yayagirlz.com and color the YaYa Girlz.

You are such a

special child who

has learned a lot.

Draw a picture of yourself.

Zimbabwe is a

country in

Southern Africa.

Zimbabwe is home to the largest waterfall in the world, Victoria Falls. It has the most official languages (16) Shona, English, Kalanga, Xhosa, and 12 others. It is home to the world's largest man-made lake (Lake Kariba). Crocodiles and hippos live there. The capitol city of Zimbabwe is Harare.

Color Lake Kariba blue, write Harare next to the star, and write Victoria Falls next to the circle.

Zulu warriors

were an army

from South Africa.

Shaka Zulu is the most well-known chief, or king, Zulu warrior. He organized those under his rule with strong army tactics which changed how people behaved.

Color his special outfit, weapons, and headdress.

Don't leave us hangin'!
Keep in touch!

@yaya_girlz

@yayagirlz_

Yaya Girlz

Yaya Girlz

www.yayagirlz.com

Made in the USA
Columbia, SC
08 June 2023

17680936R00117